An Evaluation of the Terms of Accession to the World Trade Organization

A Comparative Assessment of Services and Goods Sector Commitments by WTO Members and Acceding Countries

Roman Grynberg

Manleen Dugal

Mohammad A. Razzaque

COMMONWEALTH SECRETARIAT

Commonwealth Secretariat, Marlborough House, Pall Mall
London SW1Y 5HX, United Kingdom

Economic Paper 73 in the Commonwealth Economic Paper Series

Published by the Commonwealth Secretariat

Designed by Wayzgoose
Printed by Formara Ltd

Wherever possible, the Commonwealth Secretariat uses paper sourced from sustainable forests
or from sources that minimise a destructive impact on the environment.

Copies of this publication may be obtained from
The Publications Section, Commonwealth Secretariat, Marlborough House,
Pall Mall, London SW1Y 5HX, United Kingdom
Tel: +44 (0)20 7747 6342
Fax: +44 (0)20 7839 9081

E-mail: publications@commonwealth.int
Web: www.thecommonwealth.org/publications

ISBN-10: 0-85092-832-X
ISBN-13: 978-0-85092-832-7

Contents

Appendices

Tables

Figures

About the Authors

Roman Grynberg is Deputy Director of the Economic Affairs Division, Commonwealth Secretariat, London.

Manleen Dugal is a consultant with the Economic Affairs Division, Commonwealth Secretariat, London.

Mohammad A. Razzaque is Assistant Professor in the Department of Economics at the University of Dhaka, Bangladesh.

Abbreviations

ANOVA	Analysis of Variance
EC	European Community
EU	European Union
FDI	Foreign Direct Investment
GATS	General Agreement on Trade in Services
GATT	General Agreement on Tariffs and Trade
GDP	Gross Domestic Product
GNP	Gross National Product
LDCs	Least Developed Countries
MFN	Most Favoured Nation
MTNs	Multilateral Trade Negotiations
OLS	Ordinary Least Squares
PPP	Purchasing Power Parity
R&D	Research and Development
UNCTAD	United Nations Conference on Trade and Development
WTO	World Trade Organization

Executive Summary

The relevant provisions (Article XII of the Marrakech Agreement) and practices that govern accession to the WTO provide limited legal basis for the process. In the first stage of the process of accession, known as the multilateral stage, WTO members review the trading practices of an applicant in order to determine their compatibility with WTO rules, in spite of the fact that they frequently have a direct commercial interest. This allows existing WTO members to act as judge and jury on the trade regime of the applicant country. During the second stage, or bilateral track, WTO members 'negotiate' bound tariffs, agricultural schedules and service sector commitments, but since the applicant may make no demands, it can impose no marginal cost on the *demandeur*.[1] Due to the inherent flaws in the process, the demands on acceding countries are invariably onerous and bear little or no relation to their size, significance or development status. The general lack of knowledge about WTO accession procedures, and of documented experience, is disappointing. It raises concerns, especially among developing and least-developed acceding countries, about the costs and benefits of acceding to the WTO in particular, and the case for opening up markets in general.

Acceding countries have been pressed on the one hand to accept demands that are not required by the WTO agreements, and on the other, to forgo provisions for special and differential treatment stipulated under various WTO agreements. In addition to these so-called 'WTO-plus' and 'WTO-minus' demands, the accession negotiations also ensure that acceding countries undertake commitments that are far greater than those made by existing WTO members.

This paper deals with a comparative assessment of commitments between WTO members and acceding countries in both the goods and the services sector. It draws heavily on an earlier paper, *Paying the Price for Joining the WTO: A Comparative Assessment of Services Sector Commitments by WTO Members and Acceding Countries* (Grynberg et al., 2002). Apart from updating the analysis undertaken in the previous paper with the inclusion of the accessions of the Republic of Armenia, the Former Yugoslav Republic of Macedonia, Nepal and Cambodia, this study also conducts a comparative assessment of commitments between the two groups in the goods sector.

For the services sector, the paper compares the number of sector specific commitments offered by original members with those made by 20 other countries that have acceded to the WTO, with a view to ascertaining whether there is any significant difference between them. Using the Services Sectoral Classification List, it is found that at various levels of disaggregation, the commitments of post-Uruguay Round acceding countries far exceed those of their WTO member counterparts. At the most aggregate level, while WTO members have on average taken up some kind of commitment in six sectors out of a maximum of 12, the comparable figure for acceding countries is 11. At the 2-digit level, acceding countries took commitments in 36 sectors, compared to only 14 for WTO members. Finally, at the most disaggregated level, acceding countries have made commitments in more than twice as many sectors as WTO Members: 100 as against only 42.

The accession negotiations for services have resulted in countries undertaking commitments that apparently bear no relationship to their level of economic development as reflected in per capita income. A comparison of acceding LDC members with the original LDC WTO Members reveals stark differences in commitments: 183 commitments at the disaggregated level by acceding Least Developed Countries (LDCs), compared with only 20 by LDC WTO members. Further, it is striking that average commitments made by low- and middle-income acceding countries at the 1- and 2-digit levels have been at par with the average for WTO developed countries, and that at the most disaggregated level the latter actually fall short of the former by a considerable margin.

For the goods sector, the analysis in the paper shows that while all acceding countries have bound virtually all of their tariff lines, for a large number of WTO members the comparable binding coverage rate is very low. Apart from the much greater binding coverage, the bound tariff rate for acceding countries is much lower than that for their WTO member counterparts. The average bound tariff rate (for agricultural and industrial goods taken together) for WTO members is found to be about 43 per cent, compared with only 11 per cent for the acceding countries.

The economies of most of the acceding countries are in the process of transition; against this backdrop it could be argued that these countries have taken higher commitments to make their reform process more credible and with a view to promoting economic growth, rather than as a result of difficult accession negotiations. Ongoing economic reforms are a characteristic feature of many developing WTO members; nevertheless the commitments offered by them are nowhere near those offered by the acceding countries. It could also be argued that the simultaneous accession of Bulgaria, Croatia, Estonia, Latvia and Lithuania to the European Union could have resulted in an upward bias in the commitments made at the WTO by the group of acceding countries. Our analysis shows, however, that even after controlling for EU accession requirements, WTO acceding countries as a group have made more commitments than WTO Members.

Many acceding countries have institutional weaknesses; the reforms to which they have committed themselves under accession negotiations may help, at least theoretically, to improve their economic performance. However, when obligations are imposed upon WTO members in a flawed system, acceding countries may feel a lack of ownership of the reforms they have committed to undertake. This may result in poor implementation of the commitments. Subsequent pressures from the WTO to implement the reforms will further weaken any sense of ownership and frustrate efforts towards genuine reform. In addition, the implementation of heightened and often accelerated accession commitments is a costly venture and acceding countries may find themselves in a disadvantaged position in terms of implementing excessive obligations which WTO members with similar social and economic characteristics did not have to undertake.

This paper argues that one way to address the problem of accession is to reform the accession process. A provision for a panel of experts which examines the WTO compatibility of the applicant's trade and domestic commercial regime should be introduced, instead of relying on the existing self-interested working party system. The panel could also make broad recommendations on tariffs and on agriculture and service sector commitments that are in line with those of WTO members of a similar size and development status. Such an approach would be largely in tune with the spirit of the dispute settlement procedure of the WTO, where no member would countenance a system where panellists themselves were complainants. The alternative approach of creating an accelerated accession track for the least developed countries is commendable, but it does not address the fundamental flaws of the accession process that by their nature undermine the credibility of the rule-based multilateral trading system.

However, the probability of such reform is low. This is because acceding countries have no voice in the WTO, as they are by definition outside the multilateral trading system. In addition, the losers, if such a reform were implemented, would be the WTO members who would no longer be able to extract trade concessions from new applicants.

1
Introduction

When the General Agreement on Tariffs and Trade (GATT) was replaced by the World Trade Organization (WTO) on 1 January 1995 as the institution overseeing the multilateral trading system, it was a landmark event that would influence world trade in goods and services in an unprecedented way. Unlike under the GATT, the WTO dispute settlement mechanism's reverse consensus rule means that the legal system of rules and procedures can be enforced through a system of punitive sanctions.[2] With this newly incorporated mandate, there has been a profound change in the nature of the institution and, among other aspects, in the practice of accession to the new rules-based system.

The formal and cryptic rules of accession have changed little between GATT 1947 and the Uruguay Round agreements. (They both require what is in effect a 'negotiated' agreement on terms agreeable to WTO members.) But the actual practice of accession has changed dramatically.[3] What was for many developing countries and transition economies little more than the formal transmittal of bound tariff rates in the pre-1995 era has now become a procedure whereby WTO members in general, and the Quad in particular, use their unique negotiating position, by virtue of inherent flaws of the accession process, to win ever greater concessions from acceding countries, irrespective of their size and economic significance, in the course of their accession to the WTO.[4]

Concerns have been expressed that the inherent flaws in the accession process have resulted in the proliferation of 'WTO-plus' and 'WTO-minus' demands by members pressing applicant countries for commitments beyond the requirements of the WTO agreements. In addition, existing WTO members have hindered acceding countries from making use of such provisions as special and differential treatment and transitional periods, which many member countries themselves enjoyed (Grynberg and Joy, 2001; Butkeviciene et al., 2002). The 'WTO-minus' demands have ignored the need to assess whether multilateral obligations are consistent with the development, financial and adjustment needs of acceding countries, while the 'WTO-plus' demands have imposed significant compliance costs.

The aggressive demands made by WTO members are clearly manifested in the differences between the nature and extent of commitments made by the members and acceding countries. For example, analyses undertaken in Grynberg et al. (2002) show that commitments made by acceding countries under the General Agreement on Trade in Services (GATS) have borne no relationship to their level of economic development. In fact, services commitments by acceding countries have not only greatly exceeded those made by WTO members at a similar level of economic development, but have also surpassed those made by many developed WTO member countries.

The basic objective of this paper is to analyse the cost of the accession process in terms of commitments incurred by applicants, as compared with existing WTO members, in both the goods and services sectors. The paper draws heavily on Grynberg et al. (2002) and updates the previous analysis by including the accessions of the Republic of Armenia, the Former Yugoslav Republic of Macedonia, Nepal and Cambodia. It further extends the comparative analysis study to cover the goods sector.

For the services sector, the paper focuses on sector specific services commitments and compares the number of commitments undertaken by WTO members with those made by acceding countries in order to ascertain whether there is any significant difference between them.[5] However, a simple comparison between country groups can arguably be problematic, since such factors as level of economic development and significance in world trade might influence commitments by individual countries. For example, high-income countries are usually expected to make large concessions: consequently it is no surprise that Taiwan should have relatively high commitments. Similarly, although China is a low-income country, its economic significance in world trade might necessitate commitments in a large number of sectors. Therefore, the paper also attempts to construct a benchmark for inter-country comparison by controlling for the above-mentioned factors. It then investigates whether, given their characteristics, acceding countries have made commitments in more sectors than could be predicted from the cross-country experience of WTO members. Positive differences between predicted and actual figures can then be termed as the 'costs of accession'.

The section on the goods sector makes a comparative assessment of goods' schedules of WTO members and acceding countries to ascertain whether the latter have made deeper tariff-reduction commitments than the former. The paper focuses on country-specific goods' schedules and compares such indicators as simple average tariff rate, percentage of tariff lines bound, tariff peaks, etc. as between the two groups of countries. However, as in the case of the services sector commitments, it can be argued that a simple comparison over country groups in the goods sector is problematic, since such factors as level of economic development and significance in world trade might influence tariff liberalisation by individual countries. As in the case of services sector commitments, high-income countries are usually expected to have liberalised trade regimes: consequently it is no surprise that Taiwan has relatively low tariffs. Similarly, although China is a low-income country, its economic significance in world trade may demand a more open economy. Therefore, the paper also makes an attempt to construct a benchmark for inter-country comparison by controlling for the above-mentioned factors. It then investigates whether, given their characteristics, acceding countries have deeper tariff-cut commitments than can be predicted from the cross-country experience of WTO members. Many WTO members have reduced their actual tariffs below their bound rates, as a result of which a comparison on the basis of the bound rate alone may not be meaningful. To tackle this problem, a comparative assessment of the existing tariff regimes of WTO members vis-à-vis the acceding countries is also attempted. A cross-country model is estimated in order to ascertain whether acceding countries have lower tariffs, taking into consideration structural factors that are likely to have influenced the tariff regime in individual countries.

The paper is structured as follows. Section 2 discusses the process of accession to the WTO and highlights its inherent flaws. Section 3 deals with comparative assessments in the services sector and Section 4 with the assessments in the good sector. Section 5 offers some concluding observations.

2

The Process of Accession to the WTO

Although there were only 23 founder members of the GATT, and it was then considered to be a forum promoting the interests only of developed countries (UNCTAD, 1967), its role underwent a big change in the Uruguay Round of Multilateral Trade Negotiations (MTNs). The Round was marked by the participation, albeit nominal, of many developing and least developed countries for the first time in the history of trade talks, resulting in an increase in the number of WTO Members to 128 by the end of 1994.[6]

With the collapse of the centrally planned economies and a worldwide move towards free trade and market economies, it is difficult to overestimate the significance of the WTO. There are important economic as well as political reasons why developing countries and transition economies may wish to join. First, WTO tariff bindings can provide members with much-needed market access. Non-member countries may not have access to such trade regimes for their exports to member country markets. Second, membership in the WTO is vital for settling trade disputes through multilateral rules and regulations. For non-member countries these rules and procedures do not apply and disputes must be settled on the basis of bilateral and often unequal and unfair negotiations.[7] Third, WTO membership can provide a shield against potential discriminatory practices of any country or preferential trading arrangement; this is especially relevant in the context of the proliferation of such trading blocs in recent times.[8] Fourth, participation in the WTO provides credibility for the economic reform measures that are currently being pursued by many developing countries and transition economies to attract foreign investment.[9]

Where regimes are not stable, WTO membership also provides potential investors with the assurance that the trade regime will not change radically. Last, but not least, it may be politically convenient to justify the reform process by attributing it to external forces, i.e. to maintain that it is the result of WTO membership, rather than an internal policy decision.[10] For all these reasons, there has been an increasing demand for WTO membership. When the WTO came into existence in 1995 it had 128 member countries; by 1 January 2005 a further 20 countries had acceded. A further 27 countries are now listed as 'observers' or are in the process of accession negotiations.[11]

However, the process of accession to the WTO is much more complicated than it used to be under the GATT. This is because since 1995 the range of areas where commitments are necessary has increased dramatically as a result of the Agreement on Agriculture and the GATS. Second, WTO Members, especially the large developed countries which are the only countries with sufficient staff in Geneva to attend negotiating forums, decided to impose significant costs since GATT rules did not stipulate any membership criteria so that the terms of accession were agreed between the contracting parties and the applicant. Accession negotiations principally focused on border measures, primarily tariffs. Until 1995 GATT members were interested in the expansion of numbers and therefore membership negotiations were not very demanding. The irony of accession to the rule-based multilateral trading system under the WTO is that while it is replete with procedures, as with the GATT no rules are specified to guide the process of accession. Article XII:1 of the WTO Agreement states:

Any state or separate customs territory having full autonomy in the conduct of its external commercial relations and of the other matters provided for in this Agreement and the Multilateral Trade Agreements may accede to this Agreement, on terms to be agreed between it and the WTO.[12]

The Article neither stipulates any membership criteria nor provides any clarification about the 'terms to be agreed'. This implies that the terms of accession are to be left to negotiations between WTO members and applicants (Lanoszka, 2001) with no indication as to levels of commitment expected from acceding countries or the extent of demands that can be made of them. Butkeviciene *et al.* (2002: 2) thus appositely observe: 'this ambiguity places the whole accession process in a strictly negotiating rather than rule-compliance context'.

Although there are no specific WTO guidelines, when the General Council has received a membership application it establishes a Working Party in which the accession negotiations are conducted. Any interested WTO member can become a member of the Working Party so that it can be very large for countries that are relatively big traders.[13] Accession negotiations consist of two stages. The first, known as the 'protocol or multilateral stage', begins when the applicant government provides a Memorandum of Foreign Trade explaining existing trade and industrial regimes in its country to the Working Party.[14] Working Party members examine the Memorandum, seeking clarification of, and often reforms to, the conduct of trade practices where they deem aspects of the applicant's trade regime to be incompatible with their understanding of WTO obligations. In the second stage, commonly referred to as the 'bilateral stage', applicants negotiate with individual WTO members on the terms of their goods offer, agriculture schedules and services commitments. However, unlike normal multilateral trade negotiations, an applicant is not offered anything in return by any member country and the applicant may not make any demands apart from the benefits of membership.[15]

Thus the whole structure of accession negotiations is built on a legal system where self-interested members examine the WTO compatibility of an applicant's trade regime; as the Working Party operates on the basis of consensus, any unresolved issue between an applicant and a single member can result in deadlock and the slowing down of the entire process.[16] Thus the accession process is structurally biased against the applicant and bilateral disputes with any of the Working Party members regarding the WTO compatibility of the applicant's trade regime are akin to having a complainant at a panel act as the sole panellist. This means that any individual WTO member can impose significant costs on an acceding country in terms of demanding burdensome and onerous accession commitments and undertakings. As a consequence, a remarkable outcome that emerges out of this process is that bilateral agreements during accession negotiations may take over multilateral trading rules and procedures.[17] The legal basis for this stems from Article 30 of the Treaty of Vienna which provides that any subsequent treaty supersedes its predecessor.

Since the Working Party potentially comprises of rival trade partners and since, in the name of examining WTO compatibility, members are free to negotiate purely from the point of view of their own interests in the knowledge that the applicant country is not in a position to impose any marginal cost on the *demandeur*, WTO members have the incentive and power to extract as many concessions as possible. In the Uruguay Round when new sectors such as agriculture, investment, services and intellectual property rights were brought within the ambit of trade rules, successive membership negotiations became more difficult and increasingly concentrated on acceding governments' commitments to domestic reforms on wide-ranging issues from tariff reductions to privatisation which often went beyond the requirements of the WTO agreements ('WTO-plus' demands). For instance, Butkeviciene et al. (2002) note that under the GATT 1994 there are specific provisions for 'state trading enterprises' and no requirements for the privatisation of state-owned enterprises. Yet now major developed countries in the Working Party routinely press for privatisation. The authors further observe that while most acceding countries have to commit periodically to report the progress of privatisation programmes in their domestic economy, such an obligation is not required by the WTO agreements. Similarly, accession negotiations have witnessed 'WTO-minus' demands, which do not provide the acceding countries with the same special and differential treatment as many developing and least developed members of the WTO are entitled to receive. For example, acceding countries have not been allowed to use the 'tariffication method' for the existing quantitative restrictions in agriculture or to use special safeguard provisions for the same sector.[18]

The most striking feature of the accession process is that until recently, and unlike in WTO negotiations, applicants have been treated in the same way irrespective of their size, income, and significance in global trade. This has serious implications for LDCs and small developing countries. As no distinction was made between countries, a few key WTO members do not want to create a precedent that could be used by other relatively large and significant countries seeking WTO membership. Therefore, accession negotiations give rise to systemic demands and even in negotiating with a poor and vulnerable country, which often does not offer any trading interest, influential members of the WTO strictly adhere to these demands.[19] Recently, however, WTO

Members agreed to a simplified and stream-lined set of accession procedures with a view to facilitating and accelerating accession negotiations in the case of LDCs.[20] However, adherence to these guidelines on the process of accession of LDCs has been highly questionable.

A list of countries that have acceded to the WTO and some of their important economic indicators, together with the dates of their accession application and WTO membership, are presented in Table 1. With a per capita income of US$ 230 Nepal is the poorest acceding country followed by Cambodia, Mongolia, Kyrgyz Republic, Armenia, Moldova, China and Albania. Apart from Armenia these countries all fall within the definition of low-income countries used by the World Bank.[21] Using the same income classification, 12 countries – Bulgaria, Croatia, Ecuador, Estonia, Georgia, Jordan, Latvia, Lithuania, Oman and Panama – should be considered as middle-income countries; only one country, Taiwan, falls into the high-income group. Since per capita income based on market exchange rate may not reflect true living standards, PPP per capita income is also reported for all the countries, which somewhat changes their relative position in Table 1, but the low-income countries still have the lowest PPP per capita figures. In terms of population and exports of goods and services, China and Taiwan are the two biggest acceding countries with, respectively, 3.31 and 2.19 per cent of world merchandise exports in 1997. Table 1 also provides information on the dates when countries applied for membership and when they finally acceded to the WTO. In all cases, applicant countries had to wait for a long time, normally many years, after formally lodging their application before they finally acceded to the WTO. For China the accession process took over 15 years, while for Georgia, which had the shortest waiting period, it took just under four years.

Table 1: Some Basic Indicators of Acceding Countries

Countries	Per capita income (US$)	PPP per capita income	Exports of goods and services (US$million)	Population (million)	World Bank classification	Share in world merchandise exports	Accession application	WTO membership
Albania	750	2682	222.4	3	Low-income	0.0025	Nov-92	Nov-96
Armenia Rep.	498	1840	332.4	3.23	Middle-income	0.0045	Jan-95	Feb-03
Bulgaria	1170	4721	6277.0	8	Middle-income	0.0906	Sept-86	Dec-96
Cambodia	320	1490	896.4	11.24	Low-income	0.0175	Dec-94	Oct-04
China	710	2984	207251.0	1227	Low-income	3.3100	July-86	Dec-01
Croatia	4640	6677	8221.3	5	Middle-income	0.0755	Sept-93	Nov-00
Ecuador	1530	3255	5264.0	12	Middle-income	0.0953	Sept-92	Jan-96
Estonia	3360	7504	2705.8	1	Middle-income	0.0530	Mar-94	Nov-99
Georgia	880	3333	661.4	5	Middle-income	0.0043	July-96	June-00
Jordan	1230	3548	3572.4	4	Middle-income	0.0334	Jan-94	Apr-00
Kyrgyz Rep.	480	2310	675.7	5	Low-income	0.0109	Feb-96	Dec-98
Latvia	2300	5608	2871.1	2	Middle-income	0.0301	Nov-93	Feb-99
Lithuania	2280	6255	5224.3	4	Middle-income	0.0699	Jan-94	May-01
Macedonia	2286	5650	1393.7	1.9	Middle-income	0.0215	Mar -94	Apr-03
Moldova	500	2175	1023.3	4	Low-income	0.0158	Nov-93	July-01
Mongolia	400	1554	621.2	3	Low-income	0.0076	July-91	Jan-97
Nepal	230	1190	1279.5	21.5	Low-income	0.0125	May-89	Apr-04
Oman	6520	–	7648.9	2	Middle-income	0.1381	Apr-96	Nov-00
Panama	3020	5244	8303.8	3	Middle-income	0.0131	Aug-91	Sept-97
Taiwan	13107	15000	121294.0	22	High-income	2.1954	Jan-92	Jan-02

Note: As of 1 January 2005 only 20 countries have acceded to the WTO. PPP stands for purchasing power parity. PPP per capita income is not available for Oman. PPP per capita income for Taiwan is also not available but is approximated by that of Republic of Korea. Most figures on per capita income, PPP per capita income, exports of goods and services, population and share in world merchandise exports are for 1997. Data on per capita income (both in US dollars and in PPP dollars) and population are from World Bank (1999); export shares are estimated from UNCTAD (2000); information on accession application and membership are from the WTO website.

3

Services Sector

3.1 Specific Country Commitments under GATS

GATS requires members to undertake two major obligations: general and sector service obligations.

The general obligations, which apply across the board, include the principles of transparency and most favoured nation (Mattoo, 2000) which necessitate that each member must notify all measures affecting trade in services and must not discriminate against trading partners.[22] On the other hand, sector specific commitments, which are related to commitments made by individual members, comprise the real liberalising content of GATS and the context of these commitments relates to *market access* (Article XVI) and *national treatment* (Article XVII).

Each WTO member outlines services commitments in their respective 'schedule of specific commitments to services' following the same 'Services Sectoral Classification List' provided by the WTO.[23] They are not required to make commitments in all the services sectors and their sub-components, but specify only the sectors in which they will make commitments.[24] Since this list will be used in the comparative analysis of the present paper, it is important to explain here how specific commitments are measured from the country-specific schedule of commitments and services sectoral classification list. Appendix 1 presents the services sectoral classification list, which contains 12 broad services sectors at the most aggregate level: 1. Business Services; 2. Communication Services; 3. Construction and Related Engineering Services; 4. Distribution Services; 5. Educational Services; 6. Environmental Ser-

vices; 7. Financial Services; 8. Health-related and Social Services; 9. Tourism and Travel-related Services; 10. Recreational, Cultural, and Sporting Services; 11. Transport Services; and 12. Other Services (not included elsewhere). We will refer to these broad sectors as classification at the 1-digit level. These broad sectors can be disaggregated into several major sub-sectors. For example, Business Services comprise: 01.A. Professional Services; 01.B. Computer and Related Services; 01.C. Research and Development Services; 01.D. Real Estate Services; 01.E. Rental/Leasing Services without Operators; and 01.F. Other Business Services. Disaggregation at this level will be treated as classification at the 2-digit level. Finally, it is possible to have further disaggregation at the 3-digit level (for example 01.A.a, 01.A.b., etc.), which is the most disaggregated services classification.[25]

Appendix 2 provides information as to whether a given country has made commitments in any of the broad sectors (or at the 1-digit level). 'X' is an indication of commitment undertaken by the country in question in the given sector. Since there are 12 sectors, a country can have at most 12 commitments. Based on the information in Appendix 2, Table 2 summarises the commitments by countries at the 1-digit level.

Similarly, Appendix 3 lists country commitments at the 2-digit level, based on which Table 3 provides a summary of total commitments at this level of sectoral disaggregation. There are 55 sectors at the 2-digit level of classification, which is thus the maximum number of sectors in which a country can make commitments. Finally, Appendix 4 considers commitments at the most disaggregated level.[26] It is

Table 2: Commitments by Countries in Broad Sectors (at the 1-digit Level of Classification)

Countries	Sectors	Countries	Sectors	Countries	Sectors
Albania	**11**	Ghana	6	**Oman**	**10**
Angola	3	Grenada	4	Pakistan	6
Antigua and Barbuda	6	Guatemala	5	**Panama**	**11**
Argentina	6	Guinea	5	Papua New Guinea	6
Armenia Rep.	**11**	Guinea-Bissau	2	Paraguay	2
Australia	11	Guyana	5	Peru	7
Austria	12	Haiti	5	Philippines	5
Bahrain	1	Honduras	4	Poland	10
Bangladesh	2	Hong Kong	8	Qatar	6
Barbados	4	Hungary	10	Romania	8
Belize	3	Iceland	9	Rwanda	5
Benin	4	India	6	St Kitts & Nevis	5
Bolivia	4	Indonesia	6	St Lucia	5
Botswana	3	Israel	5	St Vincent & the Grenadines	5
Brazil	7	Jamaica	8	Senegal	7
Brunei Darussalam	4	Japan	11	Sierra Leone	10
Bulgaria	11	**Jordan**	**11**	Singapore	7
Burkina Faso	**1**	Kenya	5	Slovak Republic	9
Burundi	5	Korea RP	8	Slovenia	11
Cambodia	11	Kuwait	8	Solomon Islands	4
Cameroon	2	**Kyrgyz Republic**	**11**	South Africa	9
Canada	8	**Latvia**	**11**	Sri Lanka	3
Central African Rep.	5	Lesotho	10	Suriname	3
Chad	1	Liechtenstein	9	Swaziland	3
Chile	5	**Lithuania**	**11**	Sweden	9
China	9	Macao	3	Switzerland	10
Colombia	**6**	**Macedonia**	**11**	**Taiwan**	**11**
Congo	2	Madagascar	1	Tanzania	1
Congo RP	6	Malawi	5	Thailand	10
		Malaysia	9	Togo	3
Costa Rica	7	Maldives	1	Trinidad and Tobago	9
Côte d'Ivoire	6	Mali	2	Tunisia	3
Croatia	**11**	Malta	3	Turkey	9
Cuba	7	Mauritania	1	Uganda	2
Cyprus	3	Mauritius	3	United Arab Emirates	6
Czech Republic	9	Mexico	10	Uruguay	6
Djibouti	4	**Moldova**	**11**	USA	11
Dominica	4	**Mongolia**	**6**	Venezuela	8
Dominican Republic	6	Morocco	7	Zambia	4
Ecuador	**10**	Mozambique	1	Zimbabwe	3
Egypt	4	Myanmar	2		
El Salvador	6	Namibia	2		
Georgia	**11**	**Nepal**	**11**		
Estonia	**11**	New Zealand	8		
European Community	12	Nicaragua	5		
Fiji	1	Niger	2		
Finland	9	Nigeria	4		
Gabon	4	Norway	10		
Gambia	12				

Note: Shaded rows in bold are acceding countries. The classification of services are: 01= Business Services; 02 = Communication Services; 03 = Construction and Related Engineering Services; 04 = Distribution Services; 05 = Educational Services; 06 = Environmental Services; 07 = Financial Services; 08 = Health Related and Social Services; 09 = Tourism and Travel Related Services; 10 =Recreational, Cultural and Sporting Services; 11 = Transport Services; 12 = Other Services (not included elsewhere).
Source: As explained in the text and Appendix 2.

Table 3: Summary of Commitments at the 2-digit Level of WTO Services Classification

Countries	Sectors	Countries	Sectors	Countries	Sectors
Albania	11	Ghana	13	Oman	31
Angola	3	Grenada	6	Pakistan	11
Antigua and Barbuda	8	Guatemala	9	Panama	24
Argentina	19	Guinea	7	Papua New Guinea	10
Armenia Rep.	36	Guinea-Bissau	2	Paraguay	5
Australia	34	Guyana	8	Peru	14
Austria	40	Haiti	9	Philippines	13
Bahrain	2	Honduras	9	Poland	23
Bangladesh	2	Hong Kong	18	Qatar	16
Barbados	6	Hungary	32	Romania	19
Belize	3	Iceland	35	Rwanda	5
Benin	5	India	12	St Kitts & Nevis	6
Bolivia	7	Indonesia	15	St Lucia	7
Botswana	8	Israel	16	St Vincent & Grenadines	7
Brazil	18	Jamaica	16	Senegal	13
Brunei Darussalam	7	Japan	43	Sierra Leone	36
Bulgaria	31	Jordan	40	Singapore	20
Burkina Faso	2	Kenya	9	Slovak Republic	32
Burundi	15	Korea RP	30	Slovenia	35
Cambodia	34	Kuwait	23	Solomon Islands	6
Cameroon	3	Kyrgyz Republic	48	South Africa	24
Canada	31	Latvia	39	Sri Lanka	5
Central African Rep.	11	Lesotho	30	Suriname	4
Chad	2	Liechtenstein	27	Swaziland	6
Chile	11	Lithuania	41	Sweden	30
China	37	Macao	5	Switzerland	36
Colombia	14	Macedonia	42	Taiwan	37
Congo	4	Madagascar	1	Tanzania	1
Congo RP	10	Malawi	14	Thailand	28
Costa Rica	13	Malaysia	21	Togo	5
Côte d'Ivoire	12	Maldives	2	Trinidad and Tobago	15
Croatia	43	Mali	2	Tunisia	5
Cuba	17	Malta	5	Turkey	26
Cyprus	6	Mauritania	3	Uganda	3
Czech Republic	32	Mauritius	7	United Arab Emirates	17
Gambia	36	Mexico	30	Uruguay	11
Djibouti	6	Moldova	50	USA	38
Dominica	6	Mongolia	14	Venezuela	21
Dominican Republic	21	Morocco	21	Zambia	13
Ecuador	22	Mozambique	3	Zimbabwe	5
Egypt	11	Myanmar	3		
El Salvador	13	Namibia	3		
Estonia	42	Nepal	26		
European Community	41	New Zealand	29		
Fiji	1	Nicaragua	12		
Finland	29	Niger	6		
Gabon	6	Nigeria	8		
Georgia	42	Norway	36		

Note: Shaded rows in bold are acceding countries. The classification of services are: 01= Business Services; 02 = Communication Services; 03 = Construction and Related Engineering Services; 04 = Distribution Services; 05 = Educational Services; 06 = Environmental Services; 07 = Financial Services; 08 = Health Related and Social Services; 09 = Tourism and Travel Related Services; 10 =Recreational, Cultural and Sporting Services; 11 = Transport Services; 12 = Other Services (not included elsewhere).
Source: As explained in the text and Appendix 3.

Table 4: Total Number of Commitments by Countries in All Sectors at the Most Disaggregated Level of Services Classification

Countries	Sectors	Countries	Sectors	Countries	Sectors
Albania	11	Ghana	30	Oman	92
Angola	8	Grenada	21	Pakistan	46
Antigua and Barbuda	31	Guatemala	20	Panama	69
Argentina	64	Guinea	11	Papua New Guinea	28
Armenia Rep.	98	Guinea-Bissau	2	Paraguay	8
Australia	103	Guyana	16	Peru	50
Austria	112	Haiti	16	Philippines	50
Bahrain	21	Honduras	16	Poland	62
Bangladesh	11	Hong Kong	68	Qatar	46
Barbados	23	Hungary	103	Romania	57
Belize	19	Iceland	111	Rwanda	6
Benin	12	India	37	St Kitts & Nevis	8
Bolivia	15	Indonesia	46	St Lucia	8
Botswana	19	Israel	58	St Vincent & Grenadines	8
Brazil	59	Jamaica	49	Senegal	30
Brunei Darussalam	22	Japan	110	Sierra Leone	109
Bulgaria	80	Jordan	110	Singapore	66
Burkina Faso	2	Kenya	40	Slovak Republic	94
Burundi	22	Korea RP	96	Slovenia	82
Cambodia	89	Kuwait	61	Solomon Islands	28
Cameroon	3	Kyrgyz Republic	139	South Africa	90
Canada	104	Latvia	126	Sri Lanka	27
Central Af. Rep.	17	Lesotho	74	Suriname	13
Chad	2	Liechtenstein	86	Swaziland	9
Chile	40	Lithuania	113	Sweden	97
China	85	Macao	24	Switzerland	115
Colombia	58	Macedonia	103	Taiwan	110
Congo	4	Madagascar	2	Tanzania	1
Congo RP	12	Malawi	33	Thailand	74
Costa Rica	20	Malaysia	74	Togo	5
Côte d'Ivoire	30	Maldives	5	Trinidad and Tobago	34
Croatia	124	Mali	2	Tunisia	21
Cuba	48	Malta	11	Turkey	77
Cyprus	25	Mauritania	3	Uganda	7
Czech Republic	86	Mauritius	28	United Arab Emirates	46
Djibouti	15	Mexico	77	Uruguay	24
Dominica	22	Moldova	143	USA	111
Dominican Republic	62	Mongolia	36	Venezuela	63
Ecuador	65	Morocco	45	Zambia	16
Egypt	28	Mozambique	19	Zimbabwe	24
El Salvador	31	Myanmar	3		
Estonia	103	Namibia	3		
European Community	115	Nepal	77		
Fiji	1	New Zealand	89		
Finland	98	Nicaragua	49		
Gabon	18	Niger	7		
Gambia	109	Nigeria	32		
Georgia	126	Norway	111		

Note: Acceding countries are in shaded rows. European Community includes 12-EU countries, Belgium, Denmark, France, Germany, Greece, Ireland, Italy, Luxembourg, the Netherlands, Portugal, Spain, and the United Kingdom. Commitments are based on WTO Services Sectoral Classification (MTN.GSN/W/120, 10 July 1991) as given in Appendix Table 4.
Source: All data are from the WTO except for China, Lithuania, Moldova and Taiwan, which are based on the authors'

observed that at this level there can be a maximum of 162 sub-sectors and commitments. Business services contain the highest number of sub-sectors (46), followed by Transport (35) and Financial Services (23); other services have relatively fewer sub-sectors.[27] Table 4 summarises the main information for cross-country comparison of commitments from Appendix 4. All the data presented in Appendices 2–4 are from the WTO, except that for Armenia, Cambodia, China, Lithuania, former Yugoslav Republic of Macedonia (Macedonia), Moldova, Nepal and Taiwan, for which the authors have obtained figures from the schedule of commitments of these countries. On the whole, given the information at hand, cross-country comparative assessment has been undertaken with the data given in Tables 2–4.

It is not difficult to appreciate the problem of making comparative analyses based on the above information, as the data fail to reveal the depth of commitment undertaken by different countries. Ideally, if one knew the value of services exports at each level of disaggregation and some measure of restriction on foreign supplies by individual countries, it would have been possible to construct a comparative index of liberalisation measures. Unfortunately, most countries do not have data on services exports by disaggregated categories as mentioned in the Sectoral Classification List and information on barriers to services trade is virtually non-existent.[28] The absence of such information is a major constraint in evaluating services sector liberalisation.

As mentioned above, specific commitments made under the GATS are related to market access and national treatment, and a country can provide unconditional, limited and restricted commitments.

3.2   Comparison of Specific Commitments in the Services Sector

3.2.1   Mean Commitments of Original WTO Members and Acceding Members

Data presented in Tables 2–4 suggest that at each level of services classification the acceding countries have made large numbers of commitments. In fact, even a casual observation lends credence to the hypothesis that the average commitments for these countries are likely to be higher than those of the original founding WTO members. By employing a simple analysis of variance (ANOVA) model it is possible to formally estimate the average number of commitments made by the members and acceding countries and to determine whether the differences between these two are statistically significant. The ANOVA model can be written as:

$$C_i = \alpha + \beta D_i + u_i$$

where C = number of commitments (or commitments made in sectors or sub-sectors at the 1-, 2- and 3-digit level of sectoral classification)

$D_i = 0$ if the country is an original WTO member
   $= 1$ if it is an acceding member

α and β are respectively intercept and slope coefficient and u is the error term. In that case, after estimating the equation the following can be obtained (assuming that the mean of u is zero, i.e. $E(u) = 0$):

Mean Commitments (C_i) of WTO members:
   $E(Y_i \,|\, D_i = 0) = \alpha$
Mean Commitments (C_i) of acceding countries:
   $E(Y_i \,|\, D_i = 1) = \alpha + \beta$

A test of the hypothesis that there is no difference between the mean commitments of the above two groups can be undertaken by examining whether β is significant or not; if it is significant one can infer that average number of commitments for the acceding countries is

Table 5: Comparison of Mean Commitments between Original WTO Members and Acceding Countries

Level of disaggregation	Estimated equation	Mean commitment for WTO members	Mean commitment for acceding countries
1-digit level	$C_i = 5.63^{***} + 4.92^{***}D_i$ (s.e.) (0.26) (0.68) Adjusted R^2 = 0.28, No. of obs = 136	6	11
2-digit level	$C_i = 14.36^{***} + 21.64^{***}D_i$ (s.e.) (1.02) (2.66) Adjusted R^2 = 0.33, No. of obs = 136	14	36
3-digit level	$C_i = 41.54^{***} + 58.86^{***}D_i$ (s.e.) (3.13) (8.16) Adjusted R^2 = 0.27, No. of obs = 136	42	100

Note: D_i is the dummy variable where $D_i = 0$ for the original WTO members and D_i =1 for acceding members.
*** indicates statistical significance at the 1 per cent level. Mean commitments are rounded off to their nearest unit.

Table 6: Comparison of Mean Commitments between Original WTO Members and Acceding Countries Considering EU Countries Separately

Level of disaggregation	Estimated equation	Mean commitment for WTO members	Mean commitment for acceding countries
1-digit level	$C_i = 6.18^{***} + 4.37^{***}D_i$ (s.e.) (0.28) (0.76) Adjusted R^2 = 0.18, No. of obs = 147	6	11
2-digit level	$C_i = 16.66^{***} + 19.33^{***}D_i$ (s.e.) (1.12) (3.05) Adjusted R^2 = 0.21, No. of obs = 147	17	36
3-digit level	$C_i = 47.91^{***} + 52.49^{***}D_i$ (s.e.) (3.35) (9.08) Adjusted R^2 = 0.18, No. of obs = 147	48	100

Note: D_i is the dummy variable where $D_i = 0$ for the original WTO members; D_i =1 for acceding members.
*** indicates statistical significance at the 1 per cent level. Mean commitments are rounded off to their nearest unit.

significantly different from that of WTO members.[29]

Table 5 gives the results of the ANOVA model where the estimates are presented at all three levels of sectoral classification. In each regression all variables are significant at less than the 1 per cent level, suggesting that the average levels of commitments of the acceding countries are statistically significantly different from those of WTO members. It is estimated that at the 1-digit level WTO members on average made at least one commitment in six sectors in comparison with 11 sectors in the case of acceding countries. Similarly, acceding coun-

tries have also taken commitments in a significantly higher number of sectors than other members at the 2-digit level: 36 as against only 14. Finally, at the most disaggregated level the average number of commitments by WTO members appears to be only 42 per cent of the commitments (100) made by the acceding countries.

In Tables 2–4 the European Community (EC) is considered as a single unit.[30] Since in every level of sectoral classification EU countries made relatively large number of commitments, could it be possible that consideration of the EU-12 as a single entity might have biased the results presented in Table 5?[31] Table 6 reports the same ANOVA analysis of Table 5, but includes countries in the EC separately so that the number of observations increases from 136 to 147. Even so, as Table 6 shows, the results remain mostly unchanged, i.e. mean commitments of the acceding countries far exceed those of WTO members. The dummy is again significant in all cases, suggesting that acceding countries are significantly different from others.

3.2.2 Mean Commitments of Original LDC Members and Acceding LDC Members

It is often argued that the process of accession to the WTO has not been appropriate to the level of economic development of the applicant country. Analysis in this section is undertaken with the view to lending support to our theoretical postulation that the commitments made by acceding countries have borne no relationship to their level of economic development, and the number of commitments made by them has greatly exceeded those made by WTO members at a similar level of economic development.

Employing the same statistical tools as in Section 3.2.1, namely ANOVA analysis, a comparison is made between the mean commitments of acceding LDC countries as a group and those of the original LDC Member Group. As in estimates presented in Table 7, in each regression, at all the levels of services sector classification, all variables are significant at 1 per cent level of significance, suggesting that the average levels of commitments of the acceding LDC countries are statistically different from that of founder WTO Members.

At the 1-digit level, on average, original LDC WTO members have made at least one commitment in four sectors in comparison with 11 sectors by acceding LDC countries. Similarly, at the 2-digit and the 3-digit level, on average, acceding LDC Members have taken commitments in significantly higher number of sectors than the original LDC Members: 30 as against only seven at the 2-digit level and 183 as against 20 at the 3-digit level.

It is noteworthy that the lower the income, the greater the disparity in the magnitude of commitments between original and acceding countries. This suggests that WTO members have reversed the normal provisions when it comes to accession.

Table 7: Comparison of Mean Commitments between Original LDC Members and Acceding LDC Countries

Level of disaggregation	Estimated equation	Mean commitment for WTO members	Mean commitment for acceding countries
1-digit level	$C_i = 3.86^{***} + 7.14^{***}D_i$ (s.e) (0.54) (2.19) Adjusted R^2 = 0.26, No. of obs = 31	4	11
2-digit level	$C_i = 7^{***} + 23^{*}D_i$ (s.e) (1.46) (5.82) Adjusted R^2 = 0.32, No. of obs = 32	7	30
3-digit level	$C_i = 19.63^{***} + 63.37^{***}D_i$ (s.e) (5.08) (20.31) Adjusted R^2 = 0.22, No. of obs = 32	20	183

Note: D_i is the dummy variable where $D_i = 0$ for the original WTO members; $D_i = 1$ for acceding members.
*** indicates statistical significance at the 1 per cent level. Mean commitments are rounded off to their nearest unit.

3.2.3 Comparison of Mean Commitments between Original LDC Members and Acceding LDC Countries

The econometric analysis in this section demonstrates that not only have acceding LDC countries made more commitments than the original LDC WTO members (as demonstrated in Section 3.2.2), but the commitments made by them have been far greater than the entire developing country group of founding WTO Members, who enjoy a higher level of economic development than the acceding LDC group.

On the basis of ANOVA analysis, we reject the hypothesis that there is no significant difference between the mean commitments of these two groups. As the evidence presented in Table 8 shows, at the 1-digit level, on average, acceding LDCs have made commitments in 11 sectors as against five by developing WTO Members; at the 2-digit level they have made 30 commitments as against 12; and at the most disaggregated level they have made 83 as against 35. Therefore the measures already taken to assist LDC accession countries have not been sufficient.

It is noteworthy that the results presented in Sections 4.1, 4.2 and 4.3 strongly support a broader hypothesis: that the 'real' price of accession has been very high in almost all cases of accession.

3.2.4 Commitments by Income Status of Countries

Are commitments made by countries progressive in the sense that countries with higher income levels have relatively higher commitments? To answer this question we fit the following ANOVA model to our data:

$$C = \alpha + \beta\, MD_i + \theta HD_i + u_i$$

where C = number of commitments undertaken
$MD = 1$ if the country is classified as a middle-income economy and
$= 0$ otherwise;
$HD = 1$ if the country is classified as a high-income economy and
$= 0$ otherwise.

From the above, assuming $E(u) = 0$, average commitments for low-, middle- and high-income countries can be computed as:

Mean commitments of low-income countries:
$E(Y_i \mid MD = 0, HD = 0) = \alpha$
Mean commitments middle-income countries:
$E(Y_i \mid HD = 0) = \alpha + \beta$
Mean commitments high-income countries:
$E(Y_i \mid MD = 0) = \alpha + \theta$

Table 8: Comparison of Mean Commitments between Acceding LDC Countries and Original Developing Members

Level of disaggregation	Estimated equation	Mean commitment for developing WTO members	Mean commitment for acceding LDCs
1-digit level	$C_i = 5.29^{***} + 5.71^{***}D_i$ (s.e) (0.27) (1.56) Adjusted R^2 = 0.16, No. of obs = 67	5	11
2-digit level	$C_i = 11.69^{***} + 18.31^{*}D_i$ (s.e) (0.86) (4.95) Adjusted R^2 = 0.16, No. of obs = 67	12	30
3-digit level	$C_i = 34.86^{***} + 48.14^{***}D_i$ (s.e) (2.61) (15.08) Adjusted R^2 = 0.12, No. of obs = 67	35	83

Note: D_i is the dummy variable where $D_i = 0$ for the original WTO members; $D_i = 1$ for acceding members.
*** indicates statistical significance at the 1 per cent level. Mean commitments are rounded off to their nearest unit.

The above model is estimated by first excluding the acceding countries (Table 9) and then by including them (Table 10) to see how acceding countries affect the mean commitments for countries of different income levels. In Tables 9 and 10 the EC is considered as a single undertaker and thus when acceding countries are excluded there are 116 observations. All coefficients in Tables 9 and 10 are statistically significant at least at the 10 per cent level (except variable MD at the 2-digit level in both tables). This implies that mean commitments for low-, middle- and high-income countries are signifi-

cantly different from one to another. Combining the results of Tables 9 and 10 it is observed that when acceding countries are excluded, low-income countries on an average have 4, 9 and 23 commitments respectively at 1-, 2- and 3-digit level of services classification, but when they are included, average commitments for the low-income country group increase to 5, 13, and 35. It is quite extraordinary to find that inclusion of just seven low-income acceding members raises the 3-digit average commitment of 44 low-income countries by 12 sectors.

By similar magnitudes, middle-income coun-

Table 9: Commitments by Income Status (acceding countries are *excluded* and the EC is considered as a single undertaker)

Level of disaggregation	Estimated equation	Mean commitment for low-income countries	Mean commitment for middle-income countries	Mean commitment for high-income countries
1-digit level	$C_i = 4.16^{***} + 1.35^{**}MD_i + 3.87^{***}HD_i$ (s.e) (0.41) (0.56) (0.68) Adjusted R^2 = 0.21, No. of obs =116	4	5	8
2-digit level	$C_i = 9.10^{***} + 3.52^{*}MD_i + 16.77^{***}HD_i$ (s.e) (1.55) (2.01) (2.44) Adjusted R^2 = 0.30, No. of obs =116	9	13	26
3-digit level	$C_i = 22.94^{***} + 14.14^{**}MD_i + 55.73^{***}HD_i$ (s.e) (4.64) (6.02) (7.31) Adjusted R^2 = 0.34, No. of obs =116	23	37	79

Note: Mean commitments are rounded off to their nearest unit. Statistical significance at the 1, 5 and 10 per cent levels is denoted by ***, ** and *.

Table 10: Commitments by Income Status (acceding countries are *included* and the EC is considered as a single undertaker)

Level of disaggregation	Estimated equation	Mean commitment for low-income countries	Mean commitment for middle-income countries	Mean commitment for high-income countries
1-digit level	$C_i = 5.07^{***} + 1.46MD_i^{***} + 3.27^{***}HD_i$ (s.e) (0.46) (0.60) (0.79) Adjusted R^2 = 0.10, No. of obs = 134	5	7	10
2-digit level	$C_i = 13.18^{***} + 3.88MD_i + 13.99^{***}HD_i$ (s.e) (1.88) (2.40) (3.18) Adjusted R^2 = 0.12, No. of obs = 134	13	17	31
3-digit level	$C_i = 34.8^{***} + 14.19MD_i^{*} + 47.16^{***}HD_i$ (s.e) (5.44) (12.51) (21.73) Adjusted R^2 = 0.17, No. of obs = 132	35	49	96

Note: Mean commitments are rounded off to their nearest unit. Statistical significance at the 1, 5 and 10 per cent levels is denoted by ***, ** and *.

tries' mean commitments rise with the inclusion of 17 acceding members; adding acceding countries to the sample increases the average commitment of 66 middle-income countries at the 3-digit level from 37 to 49. In the case of high-income countries, the inclusion of one acceding country, Taiwan, increases the average commitments of 24 high-income countries (taking the EC as a single entity) from 8 to 10 (1-digit level), 26–31 (2-digit level) and 79–96 (3-digit level). The above analysis is repeated by taking EC countries as 12 separate WTO members. Since all EC members are high-income countries, their separate inclusion will only change the results in the last columns of Tables 9 and 10. The results show that when the EC countries are included separately, mean commitments for high-income countries increase from 9 to 10 at the 1-digit level, 30 to 33 at the 2-digit level and 89 to 101 at the most disaggregated level.

Table 11 directly compares the commitments of members and acceding countries with respect to their income classification. While low- and middle-income WTO members have an average commitment of, respectively, 23 and 36 at the 3-digit level, for acceding countries the comparable figures are 98 and 101. In addition, Taiwan's commitments exceed the average of the high-income group. It becomes clear that at each level of disaggregation, although the commitments of WTO members are progressive in nature (i.e. high-income countries take up higher level of commitments than do middle-income countries, which, in turn, have higher commitments than low-income countries), with average income much lower than the high-income group, acceding members' commitments are even higher than those of the rich countries. This is reflected in Figure 2, which shows that irrespective of the level of disaggregation, acceding countries' average commitments have been higher than those of the high-income group.

3.3 Commitments, Per Capita Income and Acceding Countries

A comparison of cross-country commitments related to per capita income directly would constitute a more meaningful comparison than a comparison of commitments across income groups by clustering countries into low-, middle- and high-income brackets. This would allow for cross-country comparisons after controlling for the level of development. Since an established practice in the arena of trade and development negotiations has been for rich countries to make relatively large concessions, a positive relationship between per capita income and commitments is expected *a priori*. Given this cross-country relationship, it is possible to evaluate how well acceding countries fit into the

Table 11: Comparison of Services Commitments by Income Category

Country Groups	No. of commitments made at disaggregated levels		
	1-digit level	2-digit level	3-digit level
Low-income average	4	9	23
Acceding low-income average	**10**	**36**	**98**
Middle-income average	6	13	36
Acceding middle-income average	**11**	**36**	**101**
High-income average (EC as a single undertaker)	8	26	81
High-income average (EC countries included individually)	9	30	88
Acceding high-income average	**11**	**37**	**110**

Source: Computed from Tables 1–3.

landscape. It may also be interesting to know whether the same cross-country relationship between commitments made and level of development in WTO members is reflected in acceding countries, as the range of their per capita income is very wide.

Figure 1 provides scatter plots of per capita income and number of commitments made by WTO members (i.e. acceding countries are excluded) at the 3-digit level of services classification. A clear positive relationship between per capita income and number of commitments is observed in Figure 1, although the linear regression lines which attempt to explain the variation in cross-country commitments give low values of R^2. Only about 35 per cent variations in cross-country commitments can be explained by per capita income respectively at the 3-digit levels of services trade classification. Since GNP per capita on the horizontal axis is plotted on logarithmic scale, it can be estimated that each doubling of income from one country to another increases commitments by nine sectors at the 3-digit levels.[32] A notable feature common to all these figures is that three low-income WTO members, the Gambia, Lesotho and Sierra Leone, made commitments much higher than those of countries at a comparable level of development as indicated by GNP per capita.

In Figure 2 the acceding countries are brought into the landscape. These countries are identified on the graph to locate their relative position in the scatter plots. It is observed that each of the acceding countries has offered commitments higher than the world average as denoted by the regression line controlling for country-specific per capita income. Countries such as Moldova, Kyrgyz Republic, Georgia, Lithuania, Croatia, Estonia, Latvia, Jordan,

Figure 1: Relationship between Per Capita Income and Number of Commitments at the Most Disaggregated Level (excluding acceding countries)

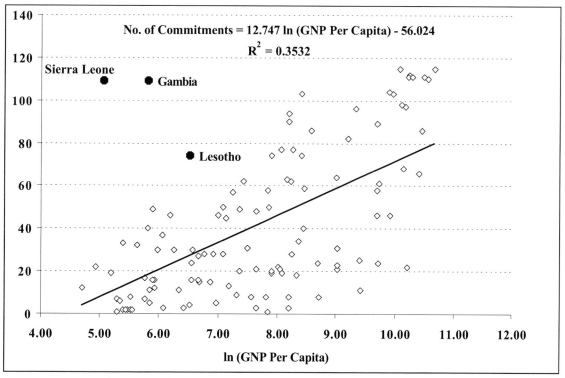

Note: Data on per capita GNP are from World Bank (1999).

Figure 2: Relationship between Per Capita Income and Number of Commitments at the Most Disaggregated Level (including acceding countries)

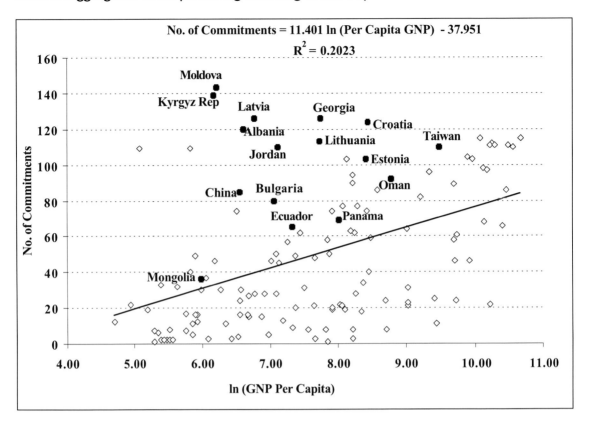

Albania, China, and Bulgaria appear to be clear outliers. Only Mongolia, Ecuador and Panama are situated relatively close to the regression line. In fact, the graph is so informative that even without doing any sophisticated econometric work it is possible to infer that the commitments of the acceding countries have been widely different from those of WTO members after controlling for level of development of world economies.

Since acceding countries are different from others, the R^2 value of the linear relationship in Figure 2 deteriorates compared to that in Figure 1. Inclusion of these countries also reduces the slope coefficients and consequently each doubling of income from one country to another increases commitments by 1, 2 and 8 respectively at the 1-, 2- and 3-digit levels of the Services Sectoral Classification List.[33]

In the case of the acceding countries, there seems to be a relatively weak relationship between per capita income, as a measure of level of economic development, and number of commitments offered, and this relationship is statistically significantly different from the one observed for the original member countries. This rather feeble relationship is exhibited in Figure 3.[34] It was confirmed that qualitative changes in the above results would not have occurred if PPP GDP per capita were used instead of per capita GNP. Appendix 5 shows the relationship between 3-digit commitments and PPP GDP per capita, where the acceding countries continue to be clear outliers.

Figure 3: Per Capita Income and Commitments in Acceding Countries

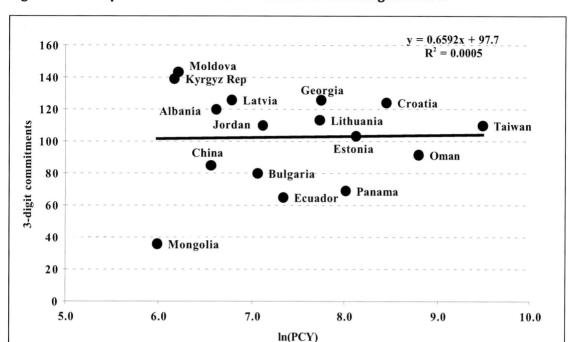

3.4 Commitments, Per Capita Income and Exports

The above figures show the low explanatory power of per capita income in explaining the cross-country variation in the sector-specific commitments offered. The reason might be that other factors are important in explaining commitment behaviour of the countries involved. One such potential factor is the size of exports of goods and services.[35] Countries with large exports may consider that trade liberalisation will be beneficial to them and thus may be more inclined to take bigger number of commitments. This may be especially true for high-income developed countries that have large services sectors and prefer the liberalisation of the services trade at a rapid pace. These countries have also made large commitments. In the case of the acceding countries there is another dimension of the importance of the size of absolute exports. Large exports of acceding countries may attract many more potential working party members from WTO countries as the latter may consider them as rivals.[36] In that process the acceding country can end up with having a very difficult membership negotiation process and may be forced to take up large number of commitments.

Scatter plots of absolute exports and commitments gave a similar relationship to that found between per capita income and commitments at each level of disaggregation of services sector classification. Thus in Figure 4 only the relationship with regard to 3-digit commitments is given. It is found that almost 26 per cent of variation in commitments can be explained by exports of goods and services. As exports are doubled from one country to another, commitments increase by a number of 7, since ln (2) times 9.46 equals 6.55. Although the majority of the acceding countries remain outliers in Figure 4, the most interesting observation is that when controlled for exports the number of commitments made by China is almost perfectly explained.

As done previously in the case of per capita

Figure 4: Relationship between Number of Commitments at the 3-digit Level and Exports of Goods and Services

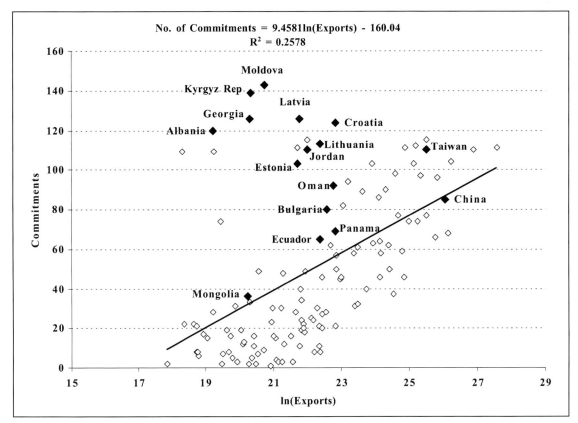

Note: Data on exports of goods and services have been gathered from World Bank (1999) and UNCTAD (2000). Liechtenstein and Macao are excluded due to lack of data.

Table 12: Acceding Dummy in Commitments and Exports Relationship

$C = -205.34^{***} + 11.28^{***} \ln X_i + 58.62^{***} D_i$
(s.e.) (23.48) (1.04) (7.44)
Adjusted $R^2 = 0.55$ No. of Observations = 140
Functional Form $\chi^2(1) = 0.06$ Normality $\chi^2(2) = 36.67^{***}$ Heteroscedasticity: $\chi^2(1) = 0.37$

$C = -229.75^{***} + 12.36^{***} \ln X_i + 410.56^{***} D_i - 15.90^* (D_i {}^* \ln X_i)$
(s.e.) (23.05) (1.02) (86.82) (3.91)
Adjusted $R^2 = 0.60$ No. of Observations = 140
Functional Form: $\chi^2(1) = 17.84^{***}$ Normality $\chi^2(2) = 77.26$ Heteroscedasticity: $\chi^2(1) = 0.47$

Note: X stands for exports of goods and services in US dollars and 1n indicates natural logarithmic transformation. There are 140 countries in the regression considering EC countries as different undertakers. Liechtenstein, Luxembourg and Macao are excluded from the original dataset due to lack of information. ***, ** and * are for statistical significance at the 1, 5 and 10 per cent levels respectively. D_i is the acceding dummy with a value of 1 if the country is an acceding member and 0 otherwise. Ramsey's (1969) RESET test for functional form, Jarque-Bera's (1987) test for normality of residuals and White's (1980) heteroscedasticity test are performed for model diagnostic tests. The critical values for $\chi^2(1)$ and $\chi^2(2)$ at the 95 per cent level are 3.84 and 5.99 respectively, which are being used to test the null hypotheses of no functional form problem, normality of residuals and homoscedastic errors.

income, the significance of the acceding dummy in the simple regression of commitments on exports of goods and services is tested by inserting differential slope and intercept dummies in Table 12. In the first regression the intercept dummy is significant, implying that the regression line for acceding countries is significantly different from that of WTO members. The slope dummy also turns out to be highly significant in the second row of Table 12.[37] Consequently, the slope of the regressions for WTO and acceding members will also differ significantly. Indeed, it is found that the sign of the slope coefficient for the acceding countries is negative, which is reflected in Figure 5 in sharp contrast to a quite strong positive relationship portrayed in Figure 4. The R^2 value for the equation fitted in Figure 5 is, however, almost zero. On the whole, it can thus be concluded that although there is a positive relationship between commitments and size of exports for WTO members, no such relationship is discernible in the case of acceding countries.

3.5 Costs of Accession: Actual versus Predicted Commitments

In the previous sections it has been established that acceding countries have offered for a relatively greater number of specific commitments under the GATS. The analysis also found that original WTO members with relatively higher per capita income and absolute exports had, in general, offered relatively higher commitments, but no such relationship existed within the set of acceding countries. In this section we attempt to determine the extent of excessive commitments that has to be offered by countries for not being WTO members in the first place, which can be termed as 'costs of accession'.[38] One effective way of measuring this is to construct a cross-country model including all variables that influence the commitment undertaking behaviour of the countries and using the estimated coefficients to predict the number of offers for the acceding countries. Then the difference between actual and predicted specific commitments may be treated as the unexplained part

Figure 5: Exports and Commitments in the Acceding Countries

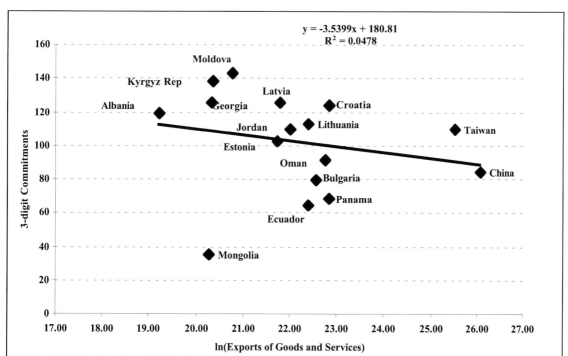

resulting from accession negotiations, taking cognisance of the experience of WTO members. Since per capita income and exports were found to influence commitment decisions by the members, and since *a priori* we do not have any information on other variables that might have contributed to it, a simple cross-country model of services commitments may be specified as follows:

$$C^i = \alpha + \beta \, lnY_i + \theta \, lnX_i + u_i$$

where C, Y, X, and u are, respectively, the number of commitments, per capita income and exports of goods and services, and error. Unlike the analysis in the previous section, this specification includes both Y and X in the same regression, which is more appropriate since the omission of a relevant explanatory variable results in biased estimates of the regression coefficients. We have kept the model in 'lin-log' form as the dependent variable is without logarithmic transformation while the right-hand-side explanatory variables are in logs, rather than using a simple linear or log-linear (also known as 'log-log' or 'double log') specification.[39] Initial experiments suggested the problems of wrong functional form, non-normal and heteroscedastic errors associated with a simple linear specification. On the other hand, the main problem with the log-linear transformation is that it makes the estimated elasticities with respect to independent variables constant or fixed irrespective of their levels, which might be unrealistic. This restrictive assumption is overcome by our 'lin-log' specification. Also, in various experimental diagnostic tests log-linear models did not perform better than the preferred lin-log model.

Table 13 summarises the results of the econometric estimation of the model at the 1-, 2- and 3-digit levels of specification considering EU countries as separate individual members giving us a total observations of 140. The first column – associated with each of the services categories – estimates the model only for WTO

members (hence there are only 124 observations), where both per capita income and exports of goods and services are found to be highly significant. However, since the first regressions encounter the problem of non-normality of errors, inferences may be problematic. As a result, the second column for all services categories introduces a dummy variable for the Gambia and Sierra Leone, DGAMSL, which were found to be clear outliers.[40] At this non-normality problems were overcome and Y and X retained their statistical significance at the same level as before. The third column shows the regression results, including the acceding countries, the resultant differential intercept (ADUM) and both income and exports-slope coefficient dummies. In no case does the differential income-slope coefficient appear statistically significant, although the intercept and exports-slope dummies are significant at less than 1 per cent level. The models can explain 32–73 per cent variation in the commitments offered by the countries.

The most important aspect of these regression results is the significance of income and exports variables individually. This means that a bi-variate relationship between commitments and income and between commitments and exports may result in biased estimation and may be problematic when the estimated coefficients are used for prediction. However, does the inclusion of both exports and income give rise to a multicollinearity problem? The estimated correlation coefficient between lnY and lnX was 0.62 – not high enough to trigger such a problem. Moreover, multicollinearity is often reflected in high R^2 but few significant variables, which certainly is not true in the case of the results reported in Table 13. There is some suggestion that when R^2 values obtained from regressions on individual regressors are higher than that obtained from a regression including all the variables, a multicollinearity problem might exist.[41] In our experiments R^2 values were consistently higher when both income and

Table 13: Estimation of the Model of Specific Commitments

	1-digit commitments				2-digit commitments				3-digit level commitments			
Intercept	-13.44** (2.20)	-15.59*** (1.99)	-15.59*** (1.83)	-11.1*** (2.44)	-64.1*** (8.11)	72.88*** (7.10)	72.88*** (7.37)	-53.58*** (9.61)	-206.8*** (22.67)	-234.3*** (18.81)	-234.3*** (19.8)	-171.5*** (25.3)
lnY	0.53*** (0.18)	0.59*** (0.17)	0.59*** (0.16)	0.48*** (0.21)	2.16*** (0.68)	2.39*** (0.59)	2.39*** (0.61)	1.83* (0.74)	6.75*** (1.91)	7.49*** (1.56)	7.49*** (1.65)	6.17*** (2.22)
lnX	0.69*** (0.13)	0.76*** (0.11)	0.76*** (0.10)	0.62*** (0.14)	2.85*** (0.48)	3.13*** (0.42)	3.13*** (0.44)	2.60*** (0.51)	8.99*** (1.35)	9.88*** (1.11)	9.88*** (1.17)	7.92*** (1.40)
DGAMSL	—	9.13*** (1.57)	9.13*** (0.49)	—	—	37.02*** (5.61)	37.02*** (5.82)	—	—	116.8*** (14.85)	116.8*** (15.71)	—
ADUM	—	—	25.44*** (4.44)	—	—	—	123.6 (26.31)	—	—	—	411.7*** (70.9)	—
Y-slope dummy	—	—	0.09 (0.39)	—	—	—	-1.91 (2.54)	—	—	—	-1.41 (6.84)	—
X-slope dummy	—	—	-0.96*** (0.13)	—	—	—	-3.94 (1.43)	—	—	—	-15.29*** (3.87)	—
No. of observations	124.00	124.00	140.00	140.00	124.00	124.00	140.00	140.00	124.00	124.00	140.00	140.00
Adjusted R^2	0.47	0.58	0.64	0.34	0.53	0.65	0.63	0.32	0.58	0.73	0.73	0.38
Functional Form	13.34***	7.56***	8.16***	4.69***	26.63***	18.89***	17.92	9.14***	22.23***	14.11***	13.05***	7.33***
Normality	18.79***	0.18	0.11	6.13***	65.79***	5.22	2.10	45.04	172.23***	4.59	1.92	77.12***
Heteroscedasticity	2.99	1.09	White	0.43	0.22	1.28	White	1.32	1.32	0.08	White	0.76

Note: DGAMSL is the dummy variable with a value of 1 if the country is either The Gambia or Sierra Leone and 0 otherwise. ADUM is the dummy variable representing a value of 1 if a country is a an acceding member and 0 for others. Y-slope dummy is related to the change in income of the acceding countries. X-slope dummy is intended to capture the changes in X-slope of the model with the inclusion of the acceding countries. There is a maximum of 140 observations; among WTO members only Liechtenstein, Luxembourg and Macao are excluded due to lack of information. European members are considered as separate WTO members. There are 16 acceding countries and thus when these countries are excluded the number of observations becomes 124. ***, **, and * are for statistical significance at the 1, 5 and 10 per cent level respectively. Values inside the parentheses below the estimated coefficients are standard errors. Functional form is based on Ramsey's (1969) test; normality is the Jarque-Bera (1987) residual normality test; the Heteroscedasticity test is based on White (1980). 'white' implies that standard errors are derived from White's (1980) heteroscedasticity adjusted variance-covariance matrix.

exports were included than the bi-variate relationship. All this means that we should not be worried about the problem of multicollinearity.

The results shown in Table 13 present one important problem concerning the functional form of the regression equations as in all cases the null hypothesis of no functional form problem is rejected. It was found that the functionality problem was removed when the models were estimated using logarithmic transformation of the dependent variables. But in that case a huge non-normality of errors problem was encountered. Although the first column regressions in Table 14 were subject to non-normal errors as well, the insertion of a DGAMSL dummy overcame the problem. This was not true when the same dummy was used in the case of a log-linear model. Thus, there appears to be a trade-off between functionality and a non-normality problem. However, as it is important to overcome the non-normality problem to make correct inferences, and since log-linear specification also has serious limitations, as discussed above, it was decided to continue with the lin-log specification. Although the above discussions are based on a cross-country sample where EU countries are considered to be individual members, almost similar results are obtained when the EC is regarded as a single entity.[42]

From the cross-country regression in Table 13 we now proceed to make predictions for the acceding countries. The basic idea is to discover what can be predicted for the acceding countries using the cross-country regression. For the purpose of prediction, the use of regression coefficients generated from excluding the acceding countries from the sample (i.e. columns with 124 observations in Table 13) will be more appropriate. Their exclusion from estimating the coefficients on lnY and lnX means that we will be comparing what acceding countries actually take up as commitments with what they would be predicted to offer, given their level of development (as proxied by income) and exports on the basis of the relationship between commitments and explanatory variables in the case of WTO members. One might argue for making prediction using the regression coefficients generated with acceding countries included in the model. However, the advantage of excluding the acceding countries is that comparisons based on the coefficients from all country regressions, which are affected by the inclusion of 'statistically different' acceding countries, are open to the criticism that acceding countries are being compared partly with themselves.

If the number of commitments is to be predicted on the basis of the estimated coefficients excluding the acceding countries, then columns 1 and 2 under each category of sectoral classification in Table 14 should be used. Table 14 reports the predicted number of commitments by acceding countries and other country groups based on the regression coefficients as presented in column 1 of Table 14 under each level of services classification, which are illustrated graphically in Figures 6, 7 and 8. It is obvious that while country groups such as WTO members, low-, middle- and high-income countries, on average have predicted level of commitments higher than their actual offers, acceding countries as a group have taken up commitments in sectors that are 43, 71 and 69 per cent higher than what can be predicted for them at, respectively, the 1-, 2- 3-digit levels. All individual countries have actual commitment offers higher than predicted at all levels of services sectoral classification with the single exception of Ecuador at the 1- and 2-digit levels. At the most disaggregated level, however, Ecuador has actual-less-predicted commitments about 48 per cent higher than the figure predicted. According to the commitments offered, Albania, Kyrgyz Republic, Moldova, and Georgia seem to be the most unusual; given the experience of WTO members these four countries should have made offers in 11, 18, 22 and 22 sectors respectively at the 3-digit level, as against actual commitments of 120, 139, 143 and 126. Surprisingly, China is found to have the lowest actual-less-predicted commitments; this can partly be explained by the fact that our cross-country model, from which the regression coefficients were obtained for prediction, explicitly controls for exports. Having a large export trade meant relatively higher commitments for China, although it is a low-income country.

Since regression coefficients of column 1 in Table 13 were used for a prediction which does not use the dummy variable DGAMSL resulting in violation of non-normality of residuals, predictions were also carried out using the coefficients of column 2. The results remained almost unchanged as Figure 9, which plots the predicted and actual commitments for the 3-digit classification virtually mimics the situation portrayed in Figure 8. Similarly the results and conclusions would have remained most unaffected had we used the regression coefficients for prediction including all countries in including the acceding ones in the cross-country model as shown in a figure in Appendix 7 that uses results of column 4 under the 3-digit classification to make predictions. Finally, we confirmed that it would have been only a trivial issue whether to consider the EC as a single unit or as individual countries. All the above results considered EC countries separately but Appendix 8 and 9 give more or less the same graphical illustration by using EC countries as a single unit and both by using regression coefficients including and excluding the acceding countries from the cross-country regression model.

Table 14: Actual vis-à-vis Predicted Commitments

| | 1-digit | | | 2-digit | | | 3-digit | | |
| | | | Actual less | | | Actual less | | | Actual less |
Countries	Actual	Predicted	Predicted	Actual	Predicted	Predicted	Actual	Predicted	Predicted
Original WTO members	6	8	−2	16	25	−9	47	75	−28
Low-income group	5	5	0	12	24	−12	33	38	−5
Middle-income group	6	7	−1	16	20	−4	47	57	−0
High-income group	9	10	−1	31	31	0	82	93	−11
Acceding members	10	7	3	36	21	15	103	61	42
Albania	11	3	8	41	5	36	120	11	109
Bulgaria	9	6	3	37	15	22	80	44	36
China	11	8	3	48	24	24	85	72	13
Croatia	11	7	4	50	19	31	124	55	69
Ecuador	6	6	0	14	16	-2	65	44	21
Estonia	11	6	5	31	15	16	103	43	60
Georgia	11	4	7	43	8	35	126	22	104
Jordan	10	6	4	22	14	8	110	39	71
Kyrgyz Republic	11	4	7	42	7	35	139	18	121
Latvia	11	6	5	42	15	27	126	41	85
Lithuania	11	6	5	40	16	24	113	47	66
Moldova	11	4	7	39	8	31	143	22	121
Mongolia	11	4	7	41	7	34	36	16	20
Oman	10	7	3	31	20	11	92	57	35
Panama	11	7	4	24	18	6	69	53	16
Taiwan	11	9	2	37	29	8	110	87	23

Note: The predicted commitments are based on the regression coefficients on WTO members only (i.e. excluding the acceding countries) as presented in the first column under each category of classification in Table 14. Actual and predicted commitments for original WTO members, low-income group, middle-income group, high-income group and acceding countries are based on a simple arithmetic average of their commitments, per capita GNP and exports.

Figure 6: Actual less Predicted Commitments at the 1-digit Level based on the Regression Coefficients in Column 1 under 1-digit Commitments in Table 13

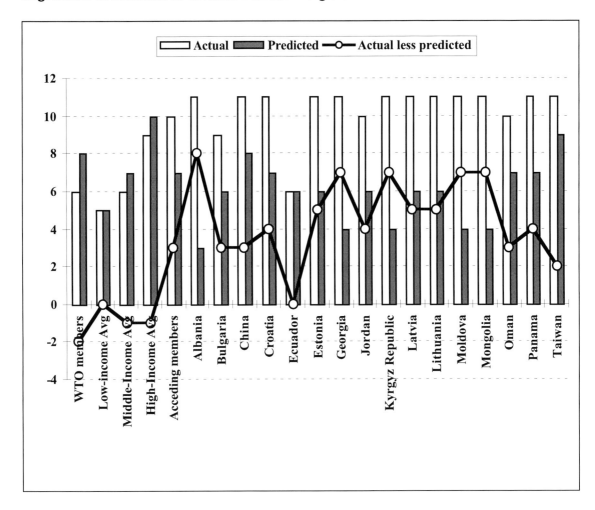

AN EVALUATION OF THE TERMS OF ACCESSION TO THE WORLD TRADE ORGANIZATION

Figure 7: Actual less Predicted Commitments at the 2-digit Level based on the Regression Coefficients of Column 1 under 2-digit Commitments in Table 13

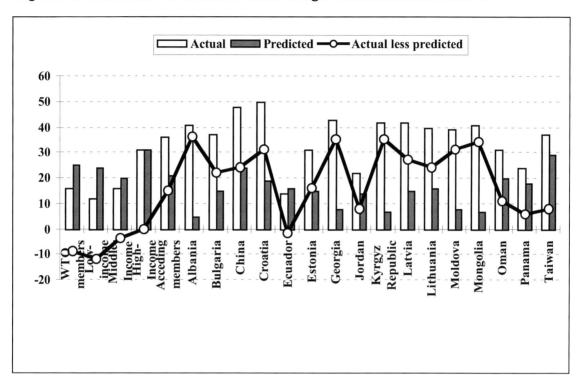

Figure 8: Actual Less Predicted Commitments at the 3-digit Level based on the Regression Coefficients of Column 1 under 3-digit Commitments in Table 13

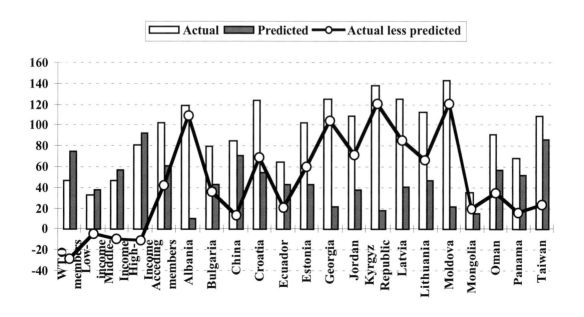

Figure 9: Actual less Predicted Commitments at the 3-digit Level based on the Regression Coefficients that Exclude Acceding Countries but with the Dummy DGAMSL (Column 2 under 3-digit Commitments in Table 13)

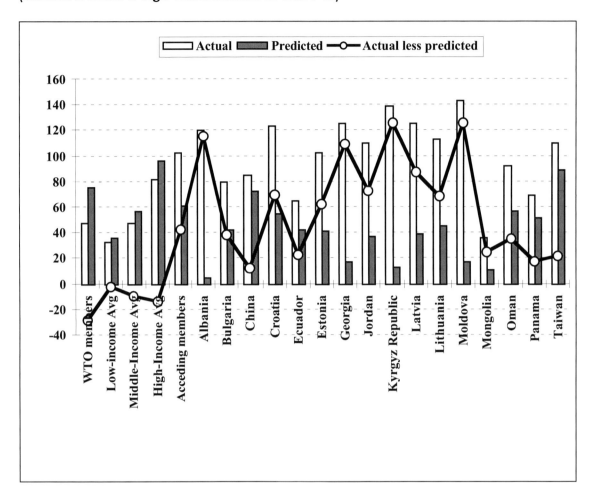

AN EVALUATION OF THE TERMS OF ACCESSION TO THE WORLD TRADE ORGANIZATION

4

Goods Sector

Acceding countries have been made to pay a high price for accession in terms of their commitments in the goods sector as well. A comparative assessment of tariff commitments made by acceding countries as a group on the one hand and founding WTO Members on the other hand brings to light some very interesting results. Acceding countries, for example and as will be demonstrated through econometric analysis, have been asked to bind almost all tariff lines in the agriculture and industrial sectors as opposed to existing WTO Members. Only 33.3 per cent of all tariff lines, for example, are bound in Pakistan (WTO 2002a), 72 per cent in India (WTO 2002b), 66.67 per cent in Malaysia (WTO 2001b) and only 13.3 per cent in Tanzania, an incumbent LDC Member.

Table 15 below provides data on the tariff binding coverage rate for all acceding countries and WTO Members. Tariff binding coverage rate (per cent) is defined as the number of HS subheadings containing at least one bound tariff line divided by the respective total number of HS subheadings of the corresponding version of the HS nomenclature. A cursory glance at the table reveals that acceding countries, on average, have a 99.97 per cent tariff binding coverage rate while the WTO Members have a lower average of 75.12.

Table 16 provides data on the simple average of the bound tariff rates for WTO members and acceding countries. Simple average is defined as the simple average of the ad valorem final bound HS 6-digit duties. The average of acceding countries is at a low of 12.4 per cent with that of the WTO members 43.4 per cent. It is noteworthy that the simple average bound tariff rate is much lower for acceding countries than for the founding WTO Members.

Table 15: Tariff Binding Coverage by Acceding and WTO Members

Country	All products	Non-agricultural products	Import markets	All products	Non-agricultural products	Import markets	All products	Non-agricultural products
Albania	100	100	Côte d'Ivoire	33.1	22.9	Mozambique	100	100
Armenia	N/A	N/A	Cuba	30.9	20.3	New Zealand	100	100
Bulgaria	100	100	Dominica	96.9	96.4	Nicaragua	100	100
Cambodia	N/A	N/A	Dominican Republic	100	100	Niger	96.8	96.2
China	100	100	Egypt	98.9	98.7	Nigeria	19	6.7
Croatia	100	100	El Salvador	100	100	Norway	100	100
Ecuador	99.8	99.8	European Union	100	100	Pakistan	44.3	36.9
Estonia	100	100	Fiji	52.2	45	P N Guinea	99.9	100
Georgia	100	100	Gabon	100	100	Paraguay	100	100
Jordan	100	100	Gambia	13.6	0.5	Peru	100	100
Kyrgyz Republic	99.9	99.9	Ghana	14.3	1.2	Philippines	66.8	61.8
Latvia	100	100	Grenada	100	100	Qatar	100	100
Lithuania	100	99.8	Guatemala	34.6	24.6	Romania	100	100
Macedonia	N/A	N/A	Guinea	38.9	29.5	Rwanda	100	100
Moldova	100	100	Guinea-Bissau	97.6	97.3	Senegal	100	100
Mongolia	100	100	Guyana	100	100	Sierra Leone	99.9	64.5
Nepal	N/A	N/A	Haiti	89.2	87.6	Singapore	69.2	100
Oman	100	100	Honduras	100	100	Slovak Rep.	100	100
Panama	99.9	99.9	Hong Kong, China	45.7	37.4	Slovenia	100	100
Taiwan, China	99.9	100	Hungary	96.4	95.8	Solomon Islands	100	100
Angola	100	100	Iceland	94.9	94.1	South Africa	96.4	96
Antigua and Barbuda	97.9	97.6	India	73.8	69.8	Sri Lanka	37.8	28.3
Argentina	100	100	Indonesia	96.6	96	St. Kitts and Nevis	97.9	97.6
Australia	97	96.5	Israel	76.4	73	St. Lucia	99.6	99.5
Bahrain	74.8	71	Jamaica	100	100	St. Vincent and the Grenadines	99.5	99.4
Bangladesh	15.8	3.1	Japan	99.5	99.5	Suriname	26.3	15.1
Barbados	57.6	55.8	Kenya	14.6	1.6	Swaziland	96.4	96
Belize	98	97.7	Korea, Rep. of	94.4	93.6	Switzerland	99.8	99.7
Benin	39.4	30.1	Kuwait	100	99.9	Tanzania	13.3	0.1
Bolivia	100	100	Lesotho	100	100	Thailand	74.7	70.9
Botswana	96.4	96	Lithuania	100	99.8	Togo	13.7	0.6
Brazil	99.9	99.9	Macao, China	26.1	14.7	Trinidad and Tobago	100	100
Brunei Darussalam	95.3	94.9	Madagascar	29.7	18.9	Tunisia	57.4	51.1

Table 15: Tariff Binding Coverage by Acceding and WTO Members (continued)

Country	All products	Non-agricultural products	Import markets	All products	Non-agricultural products	Import markets	All products	Non-agricultural products
Burkina Faso	39.2	29.9	Malawi	26.1	14.8	Turkey	47.3	39.3
Burundi	21.8	9.9	Malaysia	83.6	81.2	Uganda	15.7	2.9
Cameroon	13.3	0.1	Maldives	97	96.6	UAE	100	100
Canada	99.7	99.6	Mali	40.6	31.6	United States	100	100
Central African Rep.	62.5	56.8	Malta	97.2	96.7	Uruguay	99.7	99.7
Chad	13.5	0.2	Mauritania	39.3	30	Venezuela	100	100
Chile	100	100	Mauritius	17.8	5.3	Zambia	16.8	4
Colombia	100	100	Mexico	99.9	100	Zimbabwe	21	8.9
Congo	16	3.1	Morocco	100	100			
Congo, D R	100	100	Myanmar	17.3	4.7			
Costa Rica	100	100	Namibia	96.4	96			
Cyprus	85.9	83.8						
Czech Republic	100	100						
Djibouti	100	100						

Source: Compiled from WTO Document, TN/MA/S/4, 11 September 2002. Acceding countries are in the shaded rows.

Table 16: Simple Average of the Bound Tariff Rates by Acceding Countries and WTO Members

Country	All products	Non-agricultural products	Import markets	All products	Non-agricultural products	Import markets	All products	Non-agricultural products
Albania	7	6.6	Côte d'Ivoire	11.1	8.6	Mozambique	99.6	99.6
Armenia	N/A	N/A	Cuba	21.2	9.4	Myanmar	83.6	21.1
Bulgaria	24.5	23	Cyprus	40.4	38.6	Namibia	19.1	15.8
Cambodia	19.93	18.44	Czech Republic	5	4.2	New Zealand	10.3	11
China	10	9.1	Djibouti	41	40	Nicaragua	41.7	41.5
Croatia	6	5.5	Dominica	58.6	50	Niger	44.3	38.1
Ecuador	21.7	21.1	Dominican Rep.	34.9	34.2	Nigeria	118.8	48.1
Estonia	8.6	7.3	Egypt	37.2	28.3	Norway	3	3.1
Georgia	7.2	6.5	El Salvador	36.6	35.7	Pakistan	52.4	35.3
Jordan	16.3	15.2	European Union	4.1	3.9	PN Guinea	31.7	30
Kyrgyz Republic	7.4	6.7	Fiji	40.1	40	Paraguay	33.5	33.6
Latvia	12.7	9.4	Gabon	21.4	15.5	Peru	30.1	30
Lithuania	9.3	8.4	Gambia	100.9	56.4	Philippines	25.6	23.4
Macedonia	11.20	7.96	Ghana	92.4	34.7	Qatar	16	14.5
Moldova	6.7	6	Grenada	56.6	50	Romania	40.4	31.6
Mongolia	17.6	17.3	Guatemala	36.9	27.8	Rwanda	89.3	91.5
Nepal	24.65	23.64	Guinea	20.1	10	Senegal	30	30
Oman	13.8	11.6	Guinea-Bissau	48.6	50	Sierra Leone	47.3	48.4
Panama	23.5	22.9	Guyana	56.7	50	Singapore	6.9	6.3
Taiwan, China	6.1	4.8	Haiti	17.6	16.9	Slovak Rep.	5	4.2
Angola	59.2	60.1	Honduras	32.5	32.6	Slovenia	23.7	23.7
Antigua and Barbuda	58.7	51.4	Hong Kong, China	0	0	Solomon Islands	78.6	79.9
Argentina	31.9	31.8	Hungary	9.7	6.9	South Africa	19.1	15.8
Australia	9.9	11	Iceland	13.4	9.6	Sri Lanka	29.9	19.2
Bahrain	35.5	35.1	India	49.8	34.3	St. Kitts and Nevis	75.9	70.8
Bangladesh	163.8	42.9	Indonesia	37.5	36	St. Lucia	61.9	53.9
Barbados	81	75	Israel	20.8	9.2	St. Vincent and the Grenadines	62.4	54.4
Belize	58.2	51.5	Jamaica	49.8	42.5	Suriname	18.5	17
Benin	28.3	11.4	Japan	2.9	2.3	Swaziland	19.1	15.8
Bolivia	40	40	Kenya	95.6	54.1	Switzerland	0	0
Botswana	18.8	15.8	Korea, Rep. of	16.1	10.2	Tanzania	120	120
Brazil	31.4	30.8	Kuwait	100	100	Thailand	25.8	24.2
Brunei Darussalam	24.3	24.5	Lesotho	78.6	60	Togo	80	80

Table 16: Simple Average of the Bound Tariff Rates by Acceding Countries and WTO Members (continued)

Country	All products	Non-agricultural products	Import markets	All products	Non-agricultural products	Import markets	All products	Non-agricultural products
Burkina Faso	41.9	13.1	Macao, China	0	0	Trinidad and Tobago	55.7	50.5
Burundi	68.3	26.8	Madagascar	27.4	25.3	Tunisia	57.7	40.6
Cameroon	79.9	50	Malawi	82.7	43.3	Turkey	29.4	17.4
Canada	5.1	5.3	Malaysia	14.5	14.9	Uganda	73.3	50.4
Central African Rep.	36.2	37.9	Maldives	36.9	35.2	United Arab Emirates	14.7	13.1
Chad	79.9	75	Mali	28.8	14.1	United States	3.6	3.2
Chile	25.1	25	Malta	48.3	49.1	Uruguay	31.7	31.3
Colombia	42.9	35.4	Mauritania	19.6	10.5	Venezuela	33.8	33.1
Congo	27.5	15.1	Mauritius	93.9	18.9	Zambia	106.4	42.2
Congo, DR	96.2	95.9	Mexico	34.9	34.9	Zimbabwe	94.3	10.6
Costa Rica	42.6	42.6	Morocco	41.3	39.2			

4.1 Comparison of Bound Tariff Commitments

ANOVA analysis is used to determine if there is a statistical difference between the simple average tariff rate of acceding countries and that of WTO Members.

A test of the hypothesis that there is no difference between the simple average tariff rate of the above two groups can be undertaken by examining whether β is significant or not; if it is significant one can infer that the simple average tariff rate for the acceding countries is significantly different from that of WTO members.[43]

The results obtained in Table 17 show that both the binding coverage rate and the simple average tariff rate are statistically significant at all levels of significance: 1, 5 and 10 per cent levels.

Table 18 presents mean comparisons between WTO Members and acceding countries for different indicators. It is noteworthy that the simple average tariff rate and the standard deviation of the tariff rates for acceding countries are much lower than for WTO members. The simple average tariff rate takes a low of 11.34 for acceding countries as against 43.41 for WTO members and the standard deviation of tariff rates a low of 11.93 for acceding countries as against 19.08 for WTO members. The mean binding coverage rate for acceding countries is a high of 99.97 as against 43.41 for WTO members. The mean maximum tariff rate for acceding countries takes a high of 282.44 as against

that for WTO members which is 187.48. Table 18 also shows the results of the ANOVA analysis for all indicators as shown below. At the all product level, as well as at the non-agricultural product level, for the binding coverage rate, simple average tariff rate, last year of implementation, duty free (percentage) and the number of tariff lines with no duty free (percentage), the difference between WTO members and acceding countries is significant at the 1, 5 and 10 per cent levels of significance.

4.2 Relationship between Final Bound Tariff Rate and Per Capita Income

Intuitively, one would expect an inverse relationship between a country's per capita income and its average tariff bound rate, i.e. richer countries tend to be more open. This is reflected in Figure 10 below. However, the most striking feature of this figure is that the simple bound tariff rates of all acceding countries are found to lie below the fitted regression line. This implies that all acceding countries have a lower average tariff rate compared to the average of founding WTO members at a similar level of economic development.

4.3 Has the Price of WTO Accession Risen Over Time?

It is clear from analysis in the previous section that the process of accession has been very

Table 17: Comparison of Mean Tariff Commitments of Acceding Countries and Original WTO Members

Indicator	Estimated Equation (all products level)	Mean for WTO Members	Mean for Acceding Countries
Binding Coverage Rate	$C_i = 74.89^{***} + 25.08^{***}D_i$ (s.e.) (2.96) (8.13) Adjusted $R^2 = 0.06$, No. of obs = 128	74.89	100.69
Simple Average Tariff Rate	$C_i = 43.41^{***} - 29.22^{***}D_i$ (s.e.) (2.81) (7.71) Adjusted $R^2 = 0.10$, No. of obs = 128	43.41	14.19

Table 18: Descriptive Statistics of Tariff Profiles

Indicators	All products			Non-agricultural products		
	WTO members	Acceding countries	Level of significance	WTO members	Acceding countries	Level of significance
Binding Coverage						
Maximum	100.00	100.00		100.00	100.00	
Minimum	13.30	99.8		0.10	99.8	
Mean	75.12	99.97	***	71.61	99.96	***
Standard Deviation	33.33	0.07		38.51	0.07	
Coefficient of variation	0.44	0.01		0.54	0.01	
Simple Average Tariff Rate						
Maximum	163.8	23.00		120.00	23.64	
Minimum	0	6.00		0	4.8	
Mean	43.41	11.34	***	32.26	12.18	***
Standard Deviation	31.32	6.44		23.31	6.76	
Coefficient of variation	0.72	0.57		0.72	0.56	
Standard Deviation of the Tariff Rates						
Maximum	158.20	81.00		41.7	81.00	
Minimum	0	4.2		0	4.2	
Mean	19.08	11.93	*	8.61	11.38	NIL
Standard Deviation	20.59	18.85		7.50	17.27	
Coefficient of variation	1.08	1.58		0.87	3.73	
Maximum tariff rate						
Maximum	3000.00	2010.00		300.00	2010.00	
Minimum	0	20.00		0	20	
Mean	187.48	282.44	NIL	74.33	244.55	***
Standard Deviation	306.73	674.41		54.86	622.21	
Coefficient of variation	1.64	2.39		0.74	2.54	
Last Year of Implementation						
Maximum	2009.00	2011.00		2011.00	2011.00	
Minimum	1995.00	2.20		1995.00	2.2	
Mean	2000.9	1756.8	***	1999.7	1756.8	***
Standard Deviation	4.66	684.55		4.76	684.55	
Coefficient of variation	0.0023	0.39		0.01	0.39	

Table 18: Descriptive Statistics of Tariff Profiles (continued)

Indicators	All products			Non-agricultural products		
	WTO members	Acceding countries	Level of significance	WTO members	Acceding countries	Level of significance
No of tariff lines with no duty (per cent)						
Maximum	53.40	97.8		57.1	97.8	
Minimum	0	0		0	0	
Mean	5.08	26.64	***	5.13	26.64	***
Standard Deviation	11.03	29.18		11.07	29.18	
Coefficient of variation	2.17	1.1		2.16	1.1	
Total Dutiable goods (per cent)						
Maximum	100	99.8		100	99.8	
Minimum	0	0		0	0	
Mean	70.04	72.93	**	66.48	72.93	**
Standard Deviation	33.25	30.17		37.87	30.17	
Coefficient of variation	0.48	0.41		0.57	0.41	
Non-ad valorem (per cent)						
Maximum	84.7	70.8		85	70.8	
Minimum	0	0		0	0	
Mean	1.83	4.63	**	1.23	4.63	NIL
Standard Deviation	8.43	17.65		8.23	17.65	
Coefficient of variation	4.62	3.81		6.70	3.81	
International Peaks						
Maximum	100	78.4		100	78.4	
Minimum	0	0		0	0	
Mean	52.97	18.8	**	48.50	18.8	**
Standard Deviation	39.21	27.58		43.06	27.58	
Coefficient of variation	0.74	1.47		0.89	1.47	
National Peaks						
Maximum	11.1	10.1		12.1	10.1	
Minimum	0	0		0	0	
Mean	1.08	1.07	NIL	0.93	1.07	*
Standard Deviation	2.08	2.51		2.19	2.51	
Coefficient of variation	1.92	2.35		2.34	2.35	

Table 18: Descriptive Statistics of Tariff Profiles (continued)

Indicators	All products		Level of significance	Non-agricultural products		Level of significance
	WTO members	Acceding countries		WTO members	Acceding countries	
Simple average of other duties and charges						
Maximum	190.2	0		149.5	0	
Minimum	0	0		0	0	
Mean	9.37	0	*	8.86	0	*
Standard Deviation	25.74	0		24.25	0	
Coefficient of variation	2.75	N/A		2.74	N/A	
Maximum of other duties and charges						
Maximum	250	0		250	0	
Minimum	0	0		0	0	
Mean	21.82	0	**	18.16	0	**
Standard Deviation	45.15	0		40.16	0	
Coefficient of variation	2.07	N/A		2.21	N/A	
Per cent of other duties and charges that are non-ad valorem						
Maximum	13.3	0		0.30	0	
Minimum	0	0		0	0	
Mean	0.25	0	**	0.01	0	*
Standard Deviation	1.58	0		0.03	0	
Coefficient of variation	6.33	N/A		6.98	N/A	

Figure 10: Cross-country Average Bound Tariff Rate and Per Capita Income

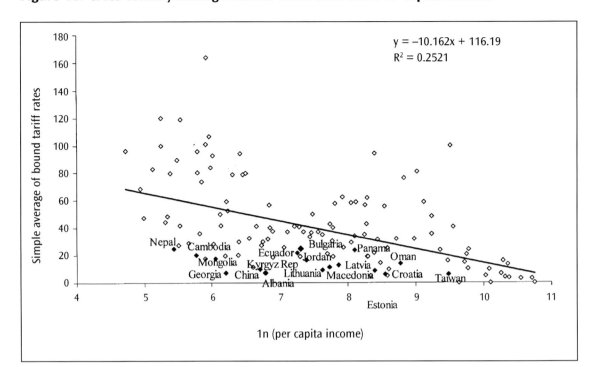

demanding in terms of market access commitments. But has there been a trend increase in the 'WTO-plus' and/or 'WTO-minus' commitments? The hypothesis that demands made at accession negotiations have increased over time is tested, taking tariff commitments in the goods sector as a sample.

Figures 11 and 12 clearly show that the average final bound tariff rate demanded from acceding countries has tended to decrease with each accession, both at the level of all products and at the non-agricultural level. The only recent accessions for which the simple average bound tariff rates have been high are the two least-developed countries, Nepal and Cambodia. The trend among the developing acceding countries is a clear downward trend.

We can therefore conclude not only that the process of accession has been very demanding for acceding countries, but also that the demands made in accession negotiations have increased over time.

4.4 A Comparison of Actual Tariff Regimes

4.4.1 Average Applied Tariff Rates

Although bound tariff rates indicate individual countries' commitments, in reality they may not reflect their actual trade and tariff regimes. Many countries have undertaken unilateral liberalisation far beyond their WTO commitments. Therefore, a comparison of actual applied tariffs between these two groups of countries may be instructive.

Table 19 summarises average final bound tariff rates and actual tariff rates by country. On examination, WTO members, on average, have much higher final bound rates than acceding countries. For such WTO members as Bangladesh, Tanzania, Nigeria, Zambia, Ghana, Cameroon, Burundi, Barbados, St Kitts and Nevis, St Lucia, and St Vincent and the Grenadines, the final bound rates appear to be very high, ranging between 60 and 163.8 per

Figure 11: Final Bound Tariff Rate (All Products)

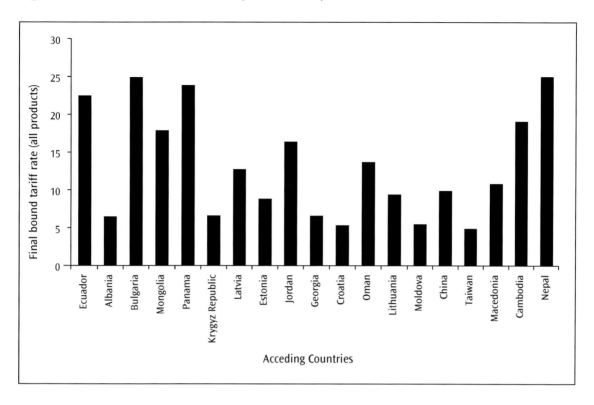

Figure 12: Final Bound Tariff Rate (Non-agricultural Products)

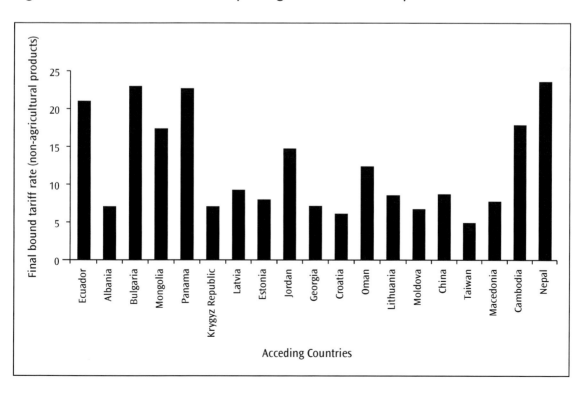

cent. In contrast, the highest final bound rate for acceding countries is only 24.5 per cent (in the case of Bulgaria).

The most striking feature of Table 19 is the big difference between final bound and applied tariff rates for a large number of WTO members. Although for Bangladesh, Tanzania, Zambia, Nigeria and Kuwait the bound tariff rates range between 100 and 163.4 per cent, their actual applied rates were, respectively, 19.5, 13.6, 14, 30 and 3.6 per cent only. It appears from Table 19 that an applied tariff rate substantially lower than the final bound rate is very common among WTO members. This phenomenon is called 'water' in the tariff. In fact, looking at the applied rates it is difficult to determine the extent of the difference between the mean applied rates of WTO members and acceding countries. Statistical analysis finds that the average applied tariff for WTO members is 10.78 per cent as against 7.86 per cent for the group of acceding countries. The difference between the two appears to be significant at the 10 per cent level.[44] There is, therefore, some evidence that acceding countries may have a more liberalised applied tariff regime than WTO members.

4.4.2 Import-weighted Tariff Indices

A single indicator like the simple average applied tariff rate may not adequately depict the tariff regime as it may understate the extent of tariff dispersion. A country could grant high rates of tariff protection to a number of important sectors along with very low or zero tariffs in all other sectors. Because of this dispersion, a simple average may result in a low tariff rate for a particular country. To overcome this problem, the 'import-weighted tariff' is used, as it is considered to be a better indicator of the extent of tariff protection than the 'simple average tariff'. However, the import-weighted tariff could understate the extent of tariff protection, as it does not capture the tariff figures for the zero tariff-rated imports.[45] To make the import-weighted

tariff measure more meaningful, Raihan (2005) has proposed a revised formulation of the import-weighted tariff rate. The aggregated import-weighted average tariff is defined as:

$$MWT_j = \sum_i \left(\frac{M_{ij}}{M_j} \right) T_{ij} \qquad (1)$$

where MWT is the import-weighted average tariff rate for the jth country, M_j is the value of imports of the jth country, M_{ij} is the value of imports of the ith commodity in the jth country, T_{ij} is the tariff rate for the ith commodity in the jth country, and n is the number of commodities. Given this traditional formulation, high tariffs will have no influence when $M_{ij} = 0$.

However, the formula used in Raihan (2005) to construct an index of tariff barriers has the following specification:

$$TRB_j = \frac{1}{n}\left[\sum \left(1 + \frac{M_{ij}}{Mj}\right) \ln(1+T)_{ij} \right] \times 100 \quad (2)$$

where TRB_j is the trade/tariff barrier index of the jth country, $\ln$ is the natural logarithm, and all other notations are as above. This index captures the tariff rates for all zero-valued imports. Suppose, in equation (2), if for any ith commodity, $T_{ij} > 0$ and $= M_{ij} = 0$, then $\frac{M_{ij}}{M_j} = 0$, but the term $(1 + \frac{M_{ij}}{Mj}) \ln(1+T_{ij})$ will not be equal to zero, rather it will take into account the full T_{ij} value. The term $(1 + \frac{M_{ij}}{Mj}) \ln(1+T_{ij})$ will only be equal to zero when $T_{ij} = 0$.

Based on equations (1) and (2) and using UNCTAD TRAINS data at the HS-6 digit commodity classification level, Raihan (2005) has computed import-weighted tariff indices for 108 countries for which the information was available. We use this descriptive measure of tariff regime to compare WTO members and acceding countries.

Table 20 first gives the import-weighted

Table 19: Average Final Bound and Actual Tariff Rates in Different Countries

Countries	Final bound rate	Applied rate	Countries	Final bound rate	Applied rate	Countries	Final bound rate	Applied rate
Antigua and Barbuda	58.7	9.6	India	49.8	29	St. Kitts and Nevis	75.9	9.4
Argentina	31.9	14.2	Indonesia	37.1	6.9	St. Lucia	61.9	8.9
Australia	9.9	4.2	Israel	20.8	5.6	St. Vincent & the Grenadines	62.5	9.8
Bahrain	35.5	7.8	Jamaica	49.8	7.2	Suriname	18.5	17.5
Bangladesh	163.8	19.5	Japan	2.9	3.2	Swaziland	19.1	5.8
Barbados	78.1	13.1	Kenya	95.7	17.1	Switzerland	0	0
Belize	58.2	10.5	Korea, Rep. of	16.1	11.6	Tanzania	120	13.6
Benin	28.3	12	Kuwait	100	3.6	Thailand	25.7	16.1
Bolivia	40	9.4	Macao, China	0	0	Togo	80	12
Botswana	18.8	5.8	Madagascar	27.4	5.7	Trinidad and Tobago	55.7	7.9
Brazil	31.4	13.8	Malawi	76.1	13.4	Tunisia	57.8	28.6
Brunei Darussalam	24.3	2.6	Malaysia	14.5	7.3	Turkey	29.4	10
Burkina Faso	41.9	12	Maldives	36.9	20.2	Uganda	73.3	8.6
Burundi	68.3	30.8	Mali	28.8	12	United States	3.6	3.9
Cameroon	79.9	18	Malta	48.3	5.7	Uruguay	31.7	12.8
Canada	5.1	4.1	Mauritius	93.8	19	Venezuela	36.8	12.7
Central African Rep.	36.2	18	Mexico	34.9	18	Zambia	106	14
Chile	25.1	6	Morocco	41.3	30.2	Zimbabwe	94.1	16.6
Colombia	42.9	12.3	Namibia	19.1	5.8	Albania	7	7.5
Congo	27.5	18	New Zealand	10.3	3.2	Armenia	8.5	3
Costa Rica	42.8	5.5	Nicaragua	41.7	4.7	Bulgaria	24.5	9.9
Côte d'Ivoire	11.1	12	Niger	44.3	12.1	Cambodia	n.a.	16.4
Cyprus	40.4	6.2	Nigeria	118.4	30	China	10	12.4
Czech Republic	5	4.9	Norway	3	1.2	Croatia	6	4.9
Dominica	58.7	9.9	Pakistan	52.4	17.1	Ecuador	21.7	11.9
Dominican Republic	34.9	8.5	PNG	31.8	6	Estonia	8.6	1.7
Egypt	37.2	19.9	Paraguay	33.5	12.5	Georgia	7.2	10.6
El Salvador	36.6	6.9	Peru	30.1	13.7	Jordan	16.3	13.1
European Union	4.1	4.1	Philippines	25.6	4.7	Kyrgyz Republic	7.4	4.8
Gabon	21.4	18	Poland	11.8	13.4	Latvia	12.7	3.5
Ghana	92.5	14.6	Qatar	16	4.2	Lithuania	9.3	3.3
Grenada	56.8	10.5	Romania	40.4	16.9	Moldova	6.7	4.9
Guatemala	42.3	6.2	Rwanda	89.5	19.2	Mongolia	17.6	6.9

Table 19: Average Final Bound and Actual Tariff Rates in Different Countries (continued)

Countries	Final bound rate	Applied rate	Countries	Final bound rate	Applied rate	Countries	Final bound rate	Applied rate
Guinea	20.1	6.5	Senegal	30	12	Nepal	n.a.	13.6
Guyana	56.7	11	Singapore	6.9	0	Oman	13.8	5.7
Honduras	32.6	7	Slovak Rep .	5	5	Panama	23.5	8.3
Hong Kong	0	0	Slovenia	23.7	9.6	Taiwan	6.1	6.9
Hungary	9.7	9.5	South Africa	19.1	5.8			
Iceland	13.4	3.5	Sri Lanka	29.8	8.2			

Source: Compiled from the WTO website: www.wto.org

AN EVALUATION OF THE TERMS OF ACCESSION TO THE WORLD TRADE ORGANIZATION

tariff rate, as given in equation (2), for 108 countries, including 14 acceding countries. Among the WTO members, India, Seychelles, Tunisia, Morocco and Bangladesh have high tariffs – above 20 per cent. Among acceding countries Macedonia has the highest tariff rate of just above 14 per cent. The mean import-weighted tariff rate for acceding countries is 8.02 per cent as against of 10.8 per cent for all other countries. The difference between the two means is found to be statistically significant at the 10 per cent level.

The modified import-weighted tariff rates (TRB) are presented in Table 21. The average TRB for acceding groups (7.6 per cent) turns out to be smaller than that for other countries (10.8 per cent). The mean difference is again found to be significantly different from zero at the 10 per cent error probability level.

4.4.3. Explaining Differences in Cross-Country Tariff Regime: Are Acceding Countries Different?

Are there particular reasons for one country being more 'closed' (or protectionist) than another? Some authors have argued that structural characteristics are important in assessing the extent of trade liberalisation (Amsden, 2000; Raihan, 2005). Structural characteristics refer to individual countries' physical characteristics over which a country usually has no control, at least in the short or medium term. Raihan (2005) has summarised the structural characteristics that have been shown to have influenced tariff regimes. These are: per capita income (i.e. the level of development of a country), the size of the country, usually measured by its population, population density, human capital, and geographical location. It is generally suggested that high-income countries are likely to be associated with low trade restrictions. The reason could be related to domestic producers being more efficient in competing and integrating with their foreign counterparts in the world market.

There is, however, a huge controversy over whether high economic growth can be achieved by greater openness or whether the direction of causality is in the reverse, where openness is an outcome of economic growth and development.[46] With regard to country size, there is a general recognition that countries with large domestic markets are likely to be more protectionist than those with smaller markets (Amsden, 2000; Gylfason, 1999).

The stock of human capital has been considered to be another important structural factor influencing a country's trade and tariff regime. It is expected to have a positive impact on the export orientation of a country, as many export-oriented activities require skilled labour. The stock of human capital can also exert a positive impact on an open trade regime; as people become more educated, they tend to want more imported consumer goods. Mayda and Rodrik (2001) find that education has a strong impact on cross-country variation in the perception of trade restrictions among people, in particular higher education, resulting in a less negative view of trade restrictions. Finally, the literature on economic geography has suggested that distance has a negative effect on trade volumes between two partners.

If the structural factors actually influence a country's trade openness, it is important to control for these factors before making a direct comparison between the tariff regimes of acceding WTO members and other countries in Table 8. For this, a simple multivariate cross-country model is specified as:

$$TRB = \alpha + \beta_1 PCY + \beta_2 POP + \beta_3 PD + \beta_4 HC + u$$

where TRB is the modified import-weighted tariff index as presented in Table 21, PCY, POP, PD and HC stand respectively for per capita income, population, population density and human capital, and u is the stochastic error term. Note that since no precise information on HC is available, the literacy rate is being used as a proxy for human capital. All data used

Table 20: Import-weighted Tariff Rates

Countries	MWT	Countries	MWT	Countries	MWT
Algeria	14.98	Iceland	3.12	Senegal	8.43
Antigua	12.17	India	29.31	Seychelles	27.81
Australia	3.83	Indonesia	5.16	Slovenia	9.84
Bahamas	0.75	Iran	3.07	South Africa	5
Bangladesh	21.64	Israel	4.92	Sri Lanka	7.47
Barbados	17.58	Jamaica	9.94	St. Kitts and Nevis	13.16
Belarus	9.5	Japan	3.36	St. Vincent	11.76
Belize	9.84	Kenya	14.87	Sudan	4.15
Benin	12.8	Korea	5.89	Tanzania	14.23
Bhutan	14.58	Lao PDR	13.36	Thailand	9.59
Bolivia	9.14	Lebanon	11.16	Togo	11.75
Bosnia & Herzegovina	6.56	Madagascar	5.17	Trinidad	4.66
Burkina Faso	10.03	Malawi	8.13	Tunisia	25.67
Central African Rep.	15.87	Malaysia	6.22	Turkey	5.36
Cameroon	13.01	Maldives	19.37	Uganda	7.4
Canada	3.04	Mali	9.38	Ukrainian	5.19
Chad	12.72	Malta	9.69	United States	2.96
Chile	8	Mauritania	9.07	Uruguay	11.96
Colombia	10.97	Mauritius	24.07	Uzbekistan	4.29
Congo	16.04	Mexico	15.25	Venezuela	13.38
Costa Rica	4.54	Morocco	25.37	Zambia	13.05
Côte d'Ivoire	9.51	Mozambique	13.79	Zimbabwe	15.57
Czech Rep.	5.64	New Zealand	3.11	Albania	11.66
Dominica	13.48	Nicaragua	5.75	Armenia	2.24
Dominican Rep.	19.61	Niger	12.5	Bulgaria	11.21
Egypt	14.26	Norway	1.72	China	13.64
El Salvador	6.27	P N G	15.75	Croatia	9.83
Equatorial. Guinea	13.55	Pakistan	20.23	Ecuador	11.11
Ethiopia	10.9	Paraguay	11.13	Estonia	0.39
Gabon	15.09	Peru	12.82	Georgia	10.08
Ghana	16.19	Philippines	3.98	Jordan	13.46
Guatemala	5.73	Poland	9.88	Latvia	2.41
Guinea-Bissau	14.3	Romania	13.52	Lithuania	2.67
Guyana	9.92	Russia	8.83	Macedonia	14.02
Honduras	8.31	Rwanda	8.08	Moldova	2.59
Hungary	8.84	Saudi Arabia	10.27	Panama	7.04

Source: Estimates are based on the information in the UNCTAD-TRAINS database as presented in Raihan (2005).

Table 21: Modified Import-weighted Tariff Index

Countries	TRB	Countries	TRB	Countries	TRB
Algeria	17.81	Iceland	2.99	Senegal	10.24
Antigua	8.15	India	25.42	Seychelles	20.88
Australia	3.59	Indonesia	7.13	Slovenia	8.31
Bahamas	0.47	Iran	6.36	South Africa	6.72
Bangladesh	17.48	Israel	6.4	Sri Lanka	7.88
Barbados	9.89	Jamaica	5.93	St. Kitts	7.78
Belarus	10.65	Japan	3.84	St. Vincent	8.33
Belize	8.8	Kenya	15.57	Sudan	4.24
Benin	10.24	Korea	7.91	Tanzania	13.65
Bhutan	12.72	Lao PDR	8.01	Thailand	14.92
Bolivia	8.53	Lebanon	5.04	Togo	10.24
Bosnia & Herzegovina	5.31	Madagascar	5.87	Trinidad	6.46
Burkina Faso	10.24	Malawi	11.01	Tunisia	23.15
Central African Rep.	14.95	Malaysia	7.57	Turkey	8.61
Cameroon	14.95	Maldives	16.69	Uganda	7.85
Canada	3.85	Mali	10.24	Ukrainian	7.34
Chad	14.95	Malta	6.38	United States	3.35
Chile	7.08	Mauritania	9.28	Uruguay	11.74
Colombia	10.47	Mauritius	21.15	Uzbekistan	9.1
Congo	14.95	Mexico	14.64	Venezuela	10.63
Costa Rica	4.75	Morocco	23.43	Zambia	11.9
Cote d'Ivoire	10.24	Mozambique	11.4	Zimbabwe	15.62
Czech Rep	4.87	New Zealand	2.3	Albania	9.11
Dominica	8.13	Nicaragua	4.11	Armenia	2.59
Dominican Rep.	14.65	Niger	10.24	Bulgaria	10.43
Egypt	16.59	Norway	2.1	China	13.16
El Salvador	6.1	P N G	15.53	Croatia	9.07
Equatorial Guinea	14.95	Pakistan	16.56	Ecuador	11.74
Ethiopia	15.33	Paraguay	10.91	Estonia	0.06
Gabon	14.95	Peru	11.76	Georgia	9.22
Ghana	12.01	Philippines	6.29	Jordan	12.27
Guatemala	5.78	Poland	10.16	Latvia	2.95
Guinea-Bissau	10.24	Romania	13.99	Lithuania	2.97
Guyana	9.13	Russia	9.71	Macedonia	11.94
Honduras	5.94	Rwanda	8.44	Moldova	4.31
Hungary	9.37	Saudi Arabia	10.22	Panama	6.7

Source: Estimates are based on the information in the UNCTAD-TRAINS database as presented in Raihan (2005).

in the regression analysis come from Raihan (2005).[47]

Table 22 gives the results of the regression analyses. In the first column we have the first basic regression. The coefficient on *PCY* turns out to be negative and statistically significant, implying that the cross-country variation in the level of per capita income has a negative and statistically significant impact on the cross-country variation in the tariff barrier. On the other hand, the coefficient on *POP* is positive and statistically significant, confirming the hypothesis that, the bigger the size of population the less is the trade openness. The coefficient on *PD* is positive and statistically significant, suggesting that a higher population density is associated with higher trade barriers. Furthermore, the coefficient on *HC* is positive and statistically significant, implying an inverse relationship between the literacy rate and tariff barriers. However, the residuals from the estimates were not normally distributed. The prob-

lem could be attributable to an outlier problem associated with Tunisia. In the next regression, therefore, a dummy representing Tunisia was inserted. The signs and statistical significance of estimated coefficients on all the explanatory variables then remained unchanged, while the problem of non-normality of errors was overcome.

Finally, the revised equation below also takes into account a dummy variable (ADUM) for acceding countries. In the final results, the acceding country dummy is shown to be statistically significant at the 5 per cent level of significance, showing that the process of accession negotiations has an impact on trade barriers. A positive coefficient confirms the hypothesis that an acceding country would have less trade barriers than a non-acceding country.

$$TRB = \alpha + \beta_1 PCY + \beta_2 POP + \beta_3 PD + \beta_4 HC + ATUN + ADUM + u$$

Table 22: Explaining Cross-country Variation in Trade Barriers

Explanatory Variables	Dependent variable is TRB		
Constant	15.08***	14.76***	13.95***
	(1.67)	(1.60)	(1.63)
Per capita income	−0.0002***	−0.0002***	−0.00022***
	(0.00006)	(0.00005)	(0.00005)
Population	.667E-8**	.6843E-8***	7678E-8***
	(.26E-8)	(.2508E-8)	(.2502E-8)
Population Density	.0034*	.0036092*	.0030721
	(.0020)	(.0020046)	(.0019906)
Human Capital	−.0634***	−.061292***	−.044964**
	(0.0212)	(.020366)	(.021558)
DTUN	−	12.9***	12.7***
		(4.09)	(4.03)
Acceding Country Dummy	−	−	−2.596**
			(1.26)
	Diagnostic Tests		
Adjusted R^2	0.26	0.32	0.34
Functional Form [$\chi^2(1)$]	0.009	0.012	1.32
Normality of errors [$\chi^2(2)$]	8.12**	4.82	5.54
Heteroscedasticity			
[$\chi^2(1)$]	1.61	0.53	0.02
Number of countries	108	108	108

Note: Statistical significance at the 1, 5 and 10 per cent levels is indicated by ***, ** and *. For diagnostics, Ramsey's (1969) RESET test for functional form, Jarque-Bera test for normality of residuals and White's (1980) test for heteroscedasticity are performed. The critical values for [$\chi^2(1)$] and [$\chi^2(2)$] at the 95 per cent level are 3.84 and 5.99, which are used to test the null hypothesis of no functional form problem, non-normality of errors and homoscedastic errors.

5

Simultaneous Accession to the European Union

For the countries of Bulgaria, Croatia, Estonia, Latvia and Lithuania, the process of accession to the WTO has been accompanied by simultaneous efforts to complete the process of accession to the European Union.[48] These countries have had to respond to the challenge of accession to the EU, the process of compliance towards which could have resulted in an upward bias in the commitments made at the WTO. Hence the analysis in this section is based on the premise that statistical comparison of commitments between the WTO members and WTO acceding members might bring about biased results in showing *excessive* commitments on the part of acceding countries resulting from negotiations during EU accession for the above five countries. The analysis in this section excludes the effect of EU accession

negotiations in the relation to both the services and the goods sectors. An ANOVA regression model was estimated to make the comparison between the groups of countries, the results of which are presented in Sections 5.1 and 5.2.[49]

5.1 Results for the Services Sector

Table 23 clearly shows a statistically significant difference (at 1, 5 and 10 per cent levels of significance) between the mean commitments of WTO members and those of acceding countries. Further, β is significant at all levels of services classification which shows that even after controlling for the EU accession requirements, WTO members as a whole have made more significant commitments than the WTO acceding countries.

Table 23: Comparison of Mean Commitments between Original WTO Members (Taking EU Countries Separately) and Acceding Countries, Controlling for EU Accession Requirement

Level of disaggregation	Estimated equation	Mean commitment for WTO members	Mean commitment for WTO acceding countries excluding the five EU acceding countries	Mean commitment for EU acceding countries
1-digit level	$C_i = 6.18^{***} + 4.22^{***}D_1 + 4.82^{***}D_2$ (s.e.) (0.28) (0.87) (1.45) Adjusted R^2 = 0.17, No. of obs = 147	6.18	10.4	11
2-digit level	$C_i = 16.67^{***} + 18.26^{***}D_1 + 22.53^{***}D_2$ (s.e.) (1.13) (3.46) (5.78) Adjusted R^2 = 0.21, No. of obs = 147	16.67	34.93	39.2
3-digit level	$C_i = 47.91^{***} + 49.56\,D_1^{***} + 61.29^{***}D_2$ (s.e.) (3.36) (10.32) (17.24) Adjusted R^2 = 0.18, No. of obs = 147	47.91	97.47	109.2

Note: D_i is the dummy variable where $D_1 = 0$ for the original WTO members and 1 for all acceding countries excluding the five EU acceding countries and $D_i = 1$ for all EU acceding members and 0 for all other countries. *** indicates statistical significance at all three levels of significance (1, 5 and 10 per cent). Mean commitments are rounded off to their nearest unit.

5.2 Results for the Goods Sector

Using the equation as illustrated in Section 5.1, the following results have been obtained for several indicators in the goods sector after controlling for EU accession requirements. At the all product level, for the simple average tariff rate and last year of implementation, the differ-ence between the WTO Members and acceding countries is significant at the 1, 5 and 10 per cent levels of significance. The binding coverage rate and the number of tariff lines with no duty free (per cent) are significant at the 1 and 5 per cent levels of significance.

Table 24: Descriptive Statistical Indicators at the All-product Level, Controlling for EU Accession

Indicator	Mean commitment for WTO members	Mean commitment for WTO acceding countries excluding the five EU acceding countries	Mean commitment for EU acceding countries	Level of significance of β
Binding coverage rate	75	100	100	**
Simple average tariff rate	43.00	12.00	12	***
Standard deviation of the tariff rates	19.08	8.97	9.85	Nil
Maximum tariff rate	188.00	136.00	73	Nil
Last year of implementation	2001	2007	2007	***
Number of tariff lines with no duty	5.1	9.00	17	**
Total dutiable goods (per cent)	70.00	88	83	*
Non-ad valorem (per cent)	1.8	0.4	1	Nil
International peaks	53.00	29	19	**
National peaks	1.1	0.84	-1.34	*
Simple average of other duties and charges	9.39	0	0	Nil
Maximum of other duties and charges	9.5	0	0	Nil
Per cent of other duties and charges that are non-ad valorem	0	0	0	Nil

6

Conclusion

The relevant provisions and practices related to the process of accession to the WTO result in inequitable membership negotiations causing acceding countries to make commitments that are far greater than those made by WTO members. These differences cannot be accounted for simply by development status.

This paper has demonstrated that:

- In the services sector, all countries which went through the WTO accession process committed a much higher number of services sub-sectors than were committed by GATT contracting parties at a similar level of development in the Uruguay Round negotiations;

- In the goods sector, all acceding countries have bound virtually all their tariff lines, and for a large number of WTO members the comparable binding coverage is very low.

In the services sector, it has been found that at each level of services sectoral classification, the commitments of acceding countries were far greater than those made by WTO members. At the most aggregate level, on average, while WTO countries were found to have some commitment in six sectors, out of a maximum of 12, the comparable figure for WTO acceding countries is 11. At the 2-digit level, acceding countries made commitments in 36 sectors compared to only 14 of the original WTO members. Finally, at the most disaggregated level, acceding countries have commitments more than twice as great as WTO Members; 100 as against only 42. In every case the difference in mean commitments between the two groups is statistically significant.

Taking all countries together, a positive relationship between per capita income and number of sector specific commitments is observed, but it becomes obvious that each acceding country has offered commitments higher than the world average, controlling for country specific level of development. Besides, the relationship between per capita income and commitment in the set of acceding countries alone turns out to be random, i.e. there is no significant relationship between income and commitments. A positive relationship between exports and commitments has also been found among the countries; with the exception of China all other acceding countries were found to lie above the cross-country regression line. But again, no statistically significant relationship between exports and service sector commitments was found in the sample of acceding countries.

Taking into consideration the level of economic development and the volume of exports of good and services, when the cross-country experience of commitment offering behaviour of WTO members is used to predict the outcomes for acceding countries, it is found that the actual commitments in every case is higher than the figures predicted. The results indicate that if Lithuania, Kyrgyz Republic, Albania and Georgia were original WTO founder members, they would have commitments at least as low as 15 per cent of what they actually undertook during accession.

In the goods sector, apart from the much greater binding coverage rate, the bound tariff rate for acceding countries is much lower than that for their WTO member counterparts. The average bound tariff rate (for both agricultural and industrial goods taken together) for WTO members is found to be about 43 per cent, in comparison with just 11 per cent for the acceding countries.

It follows that while the WTO members have considerable leeway in terms of the capacity of upward adjustment of their tariff regime, whenever this becomes a necessary policy decision, for acceding countries similar actions will probably be WTO inconsistent. In this context, acceding countries are in a greatly disadvantaged position vis-à-vis WTO members.

Despite very high bound rates, most WTO members have substantially reduced their actual applied tariff rates. Nevertheless, the analysis presented in this paper suggests that, even in terms of applied rates, acceding countries have smaller average tariffs than the WTO members. Several structural factors influence the cross-country variation in tariff rates; even after controlling for these factors, acceding countries have been found to have lower average tariff rates.

It is acknowledged that lower tariffs are not necessarily bad, and are considered the principal source of static welfare gains for an economy undertaking trade liberalisation measures. However, the point being made here is that while WTO members have had the flexibility of keeping their bound tariff rates at a high level, through a structurally inequitable process of accession negotiations, the acceding countries have been compelled to lower their bound rates.

Most of the acceding countries are economies that are in the process of a transition; against this backdrop it could be argued that these countries had taken on higher commitments to make their reform process more credible and to promote economic growth, rather than as a result of difficult accession negotiations. While it is true that most acceding countries are serious about reform and no distinction can be made between commitments offered as a result of accession negotiations and willingness to undertake genuine reforms, the very long time period associated with accession negotia-

tions seem to suggest that pressure from WTO members is likely to have been the most significant factor in acceding countries' conceding higher commitments. Besides, ongoing economic reforms are characteristic features of many developing WTO members; nevertheless, the commitments offered by them (in terms of services sub-sectors, bound tariff rates for goods and percentage of tariff lines bound) are nowhere near those offered by the acceding countries. Furthermore, the exclusion of acceding countries from the provision of special and differential treatment and the imposition of demands that go beyond the requirements of WTO agreements reveal the discriminatory and extremely demanding characteristics of accession process.

Very importantly, it could be argued that WTO acceding countries as a group demonstrate higher commitments on account of the stringent accession requirements for the five countries simultaneously acceding to the EU – Bulgaria, Croatia, Estonia, Latvia and Lithuania. The paper has presented statistics which show that even after controlling for EU accession requirements, WTO acceding countries as a group have made more commitments than WTO Members.

Despite all the benefits of WTO membership there is no denying that accession is a costly venture, even in an absolute sense, in terms of opportunity costs of employing highly skilled personnel for active participation in WTO negotiations and the resources required for the implementation of the commitments made (Langhammer and Lucke, 2001). Implementation requires training of personnel, purchase of machinery and equipment, and often the introduction of new systems and procedures. Evidence suggests that these costs can be substantial.[50] As a result, most acceding countries are likely to find it very difficult to fulfil the obligations and commitments they have made during accession negotiations, which many WTO members with similar social and economic characteristics did not have to undertake. The problem may be more acute for acceding LDCs.

It may be true that there are institutional weaknesses in many acceding countries and that reforms, as committed to under the accession negotiations, will actually benefit them. But when commitments are imposed by some WTO members through unequal accession negotiations, acceding countries may not sense the ownership of the reforms that they are supposed to implement.[51] Lack of demand for reforms from the domestic economy can result in poor implementation of the commitment programmes and inadequate utilisation of costly resources used in them irrespective of whether these activities are supported by domestic efforts or foreign assistance. Under such circumstances, as Finger and Schuler (2000: 513) appositely observe:

> ... attempts to force implementation through the WTO settlement mechanism would likely reinforce the impression that the WTO rules are imperially imposed from the outside, for the benefit of the outside.

This will result in further loss of the sense of ownership. This is precisely why the most often heard argument that reforms to be undertaken through the accession negotiations are to benefit the acceding countries substantially is simply overstated and hardly corresponds to the reality of these economies or of the actual process of accession.

One way to alleviate the problems is to reform the accession process. A provision for a panel of experts examining the WTO compatibility of the applicant's trade and industrial regime could be introduced instead of the self-interested Working Party system. The panel could produce a formal report to the WTO, which could then act as the basis of further negotiations. This is largely in line with the dispute settlement procedure of the WTO where no member would countenance a system where panellists themselves were complainants. Alternatively, at the very least, vulnerable small states should be allowed to have easy entry into the WTO and to access the same special and differential treatment as is enjoyed by other WTO LDC members. However, such an initiative to reform the process of accession to the WTO may never be introduced. This is because acceding countries do not have any voice in the WTO, as they are by definition outside the multilateral trading system. In addition, the losers from such a reform will be WTO members who would no longer be able to extract trade concessions from applicants. Therefore, even the poor and most vulnerable economies may have to continue paying a belated price for joining the WTO.

Notes

1 Besides the marginal cost of not providing market access to WTO Members.

2 Under the GATT, adoption of a panel report required consensus amongst all members and hence the unsuccessful disputant could block the adoption of any panel report.

3 Article XXXIII (GATT 1947) and Article 12 of the Marrakech Agreement define the terms of accession under the GATT and WTO Agreements.

4 The commitments related to services trade began to be offered by countries only in the Uruguay Round, when rules for such trading were introduced under the General Agreements on Trade in Services. The Quad comprises the US, the EU, Japan and Canada.

5 A similar analysis for the goods sector could be undertaken on the basis of pre- and post-membership tariff barriers. However, although data on tariff bindings for the acceding countries are available, such information on WTO members is not released in electronic format. They are available in a country-specific schedule of commitments and are published in printed format only. Therefore, compiling the information for cross-country comparison is extremely time-consuming and has been left for future research. Nonetheless, there are clear indications that the liberalisation commitments made by acceding countries in the goods sector are enormous. For example, most, if not all, of them have bound tariffs on all items of agricultural and non-agricultural products and simple average of individual tariff bindings range between 5–15 per cent only (WTO, 2000).

6 This section of the paper draws heavily on Grynberg *et al.* (2002).

7 When a country is not a member of the WTO, trade disputes involving it have to be settled through complex bilateral negotiations, which are unlikely to follow WTO rules and procedures. Among others, China experienced this kind of difficulty, resulting in considerable market access barriers especially to the US because of unilateral action imposed by the latter. It is not only developed countries which have used unilateral measures at the expense of non-member countries; many developing countries have also adopted such practices. One often cited example is the decision by the Mexican Government to impose anti-dumping duties on all Chinese goods and to increase its tariffs by 300–1000 per cent in 1993 (Yang, 1999). Having obtained WTO membership, acceding countries will potentially be able to challenge such trade restrictive measures at the WTO.

8 Since 1948 as many as 200 preferential trading blocs have been notified to the GATT or the WTO; approximately 50 per cent of these have been in the 1990s (Hoekman and Kostecki, 2001: 346).

9 In fact, accession to the WTO has become increasingly important as an internal policy instrument locking in systemic reforms of the acceding country. One of the traditional policy clichés of the GATT was the analogy drawn between the binding of tariffs and the Homeric Myth of Ulysses and the Sirens when Ulysses, in order to hear the call of the Sirens, asks that his arms be bound to the mast. In the analogy, the mast is the GATT, the bindings are tariff bindings and the Sirens are the public, which demands protection from the policy makers.

10 Especially when reforms are very costly in terms of financial resources or job losses, demand for internal policy decisions for such actions does not exist. For example, according to one estimate the reforms of the Chinese economy that have been agreed during the WTO accession process will result in 12 million job losses in industry and 13 million in agriculture by 2006 (Nomura Asia, *Economic Insight*, 12 December 2001).

11 The figure of 144 members includes both the EC and its individual members. Without the EC, the WTO has 143 members. The list of 16 acceding countries is given in Table 1. Many 'observer' countries have formally lodged their applications to join the WTO and are now negotiating with their respective working party groups. According to WTO procedures, observers must start accession negotiations within five years of becoming observers. Currently, the observers are Algeria, Armenia, Andorra, Azerbaijan, the Bahamas, Belarus, Bhutan, Bosnia and Herzegovina, Cambodia, Cape Verde, Equatorial Guinea, Ethiopia, Former Yugoslav Republic of Macedonia, Kazakhstan, Lao PDR, Lebanon, Nepal, Russian, Federation, Samoa, Sao Tome Principe, Saudi Arabia, Seychelles, Sudan, Tajikistan, Tonga, Ukraine, Uzbekistan, Vanuatu, Vietnam, Yemen and Federal Republic of Yugoslavia.

12 See *The Legal Texts – The Results of the Uruguay Round of Multilateral Trade Negotiations*. The texts can also be found on the official website of the WTO at http//www.wto.org.

13 For example, in the case of China the working party consisted of 74 members.

14 This Memorandum is usually accompanied by other documents such as the currently applicable tariff schedule at detailed commodity classification levels, information on domestic support for the agriculture sector, export subsidies and list of commitments, both in the goods as well as in the services sectors, that the applicant is willing to undertake.

15 Details on the process of accession are available in Grynberg and Joy (2000) and Lanoszka (2001).

16 Under WTO accession the membership is legally based on a vote of two-thirds majority in the Minis-

terial Conference (MC), but in practice the negotiations with the Working Party precede the decisions of the MC. The Working Party acts on the basis of the consensus principle, resulting in any unsatisfied member's blocking the negotiations. For instance, although all the Quad countries were important players, the bilateral negotiations between the US and China acted as the principal factor in the latter's accession to the WTO (Wei, 1999). After nearly 14 years of tortuous parley, it was only when Sino-US negotiations reached a successful conclusion that the prospect of China's membership became a reality (Yang, 2000).

17 For example, entry into the multilateral trading system will not protect China from unilateral actions by the US, as agreed under Sino-US negotiations and embodied in the draft protocol of its accession. Yang (2000) points out three remarkable aspects of the protocol that show how even after accession to the WTO bilateral actions can be influential. Firstly, for the purpose of anti-dumping and countervailing measures the US will be able to treat China as a non-market economy and will retain the right to use third country reference prices when disputes arise. This practice will remain effective for 15 years after China's accession to the WTO. Secondly, using product specific safeguard measures the US will be able to unilaterally restrict Chinese exports based on standards that are lower than WTO provisions; this exclusive US safeguard mechanism will last for 12 years following China's accession. And thirdly, even after the phasing out of the MFA quota in 2004, the US will be able to restrict imports of textiles and clothing from China until 2008.

18 Butkeviciene et al. (2002) cite a number of 'WTO-plus' and 'WTO-minus' demands negotiated with acceding countries. The authors observe: '… resistance to include S&D (special and differential) in the terms of accession is in sharp contrast with the thrust of the Doha Ministerial Declaration and the Ministerial Decision on Implementation-Related Issues and Concerns'.

19 Even in the case of a small vulnerable island state such as Vanuatu, which does not attract any significant bilateral trading interest, the US placed very rigorous systemic demands, including rapid liberalisation of trade regime, acceptance of the Agreement on Government Procurement and the Agreement on Civil Aircraft (Grynberg and Joy, 1999). While liberalisation programmes implemented under systemic bindings in a relatively open economy may facilitate investment and development, there is no assurance that many of the far-reaching market opening demands of WTO members on acceding countries are necessarily in the long-term development interests of

those acceding countries, especially of small and vulnerable states.

20 Refer to WTO document WT/COMTD/LDC/12.

21 According to the World Bank, low–income countries are those that had a per capita income of or less than US$785 in 1997. Countries with a per capita income higher than US$785 but less than or equal to US$9656 are classified as middle-income. High-income economies are those with a per capita of US$9656 or more.

22 GATS, however, has a provision that allows members to list temporary exemptions to MFN.

23 This list was prepared by the WTO. The reference for WTO documentation is MTN.GNS/W/120, 10 July 1991. Schedules of specific commitments for all countries are available on the WTO website: http://www.wto.org.

24 This essentially implies that if any sector is not listed in a country's national schedule then it is not undertaking any commitment related to that sector.

25 Only in two instances is it possible to have disaggregation at the 4-digit level. These are 02.C.o and 07.B.f.

26 Note that although this level of classification will be called the 3-digit level, for sub-sectors 02.C.o and 07.B.f the commitments are counted at the 4-digit level.

27 There is no disaggregated information for Sector 12 (Services not included elsewhere) and thus the sector is excluded from the counts in Appendix Table 4. This should hardly make any difference as Appendix 2 shows that there are only eight countries that have made commitments under this category. Moreover, any further disaggregation (for example at 2- or 3-digit level) for this sector is unavailable.

28 As Karsenty (2000: 33) observes: 'The General Agreement on Trade in Services (GATS) was concluded during the Uruguay Round of trade negotiations without the support of relevant statistical information'.

29 While the significance of the coefficient on the dummy variable will confirm that acceding countries are different from members, a positive sign on the coefficient will imply that the average number of commitments for the former is higher than that for the latter.

30 The unit includes 12 countries: Belgium, Denmark, France, Germany, Greece, Ireland, Italy, Luxembourg, the Netherlands, Portugal, Spain and the United Kingdom. Information on the other three EU members (Finland, Norway and Sweden) is given separately in Tables 1–3.

31 This question arises because the EC has commitments higher than the average of the acceding countries in all cases, as reported in Tables 1–3.

32 This is estimated as, for example, at the 3-digit level, $\ln(2) \times 12.747 = 8.83$. Since the number of commit-

ments are in whole numbers the fractions are rounded off to their nearest unit.

33 Due to rounding-off no reduction of commitments is found at the 1-digit level.

34 The estimated R^2 for the relationship in Figure 8 is very close to zero, which further reveals that the distribution of commitments for acceding countries over their per capita income is random.

35 We will consider absolute size of exports rather than export-propensity or export-GDP ratio. This is because export-GDP ratio can conceal the actual capacity to export and level of development. For example, Djibouti's export-GDP ratio is more than double that of China, but this does not mean anything useful in cross-country comparisons. Another example is that despite having a similar export-ratio, China's absolute exports are 90 times greater than those of Cameroon. Similarly, the two largest exporters in the world, the US and Japan, have the lowest export-GDP ratios of 11.6 and 9.9 per cent, respectively, in world economies. Countries with small populations are more likely to depend on their external trade, but do not necessarily have a high income. Such a trend may not be found in large rich countries (see Gylfason, 1999). Appendix 6 provides the scatter plot of export-GDP ratio and commitments for 124 countries, where it is found that the scatters are almost random and the estimated fit of the linear regression line is almost equal to zero.

36 To some extent this certainly happened to the accession process of China, which has one of the biggest export sectors in the world economy and the highest number of working party members negotiating on its accession request.

37 However, diagnostic tests suggest that in both regressions of Table 13 the assumption of normality of residuals is violated, in which case inferences drawn may not be valid. The problem of non-normality of residuals was found to be caused by large commitments of the Gambia and Sierra Leone. A dummy variable representing these two countries eliminated the problem of non-normality of errors. At this, all the variables remained significant at less than one per cent level and coefficients on the intercept, $\ln X_i$, D_i and $D_i*\ln X_i$ in the second regression were computed to be, respectively, −256.68, 13.57, 439.50 and −17.11. The coefficient on the dummy for the Gambia and Sierra Leone was 112.59 and was also significant at the 1 per cent level. The adjusted R^2 for this equation rose to 0.70. On the whole, these results confirm that the non-normality problem would not have biased the inferences drawn on the basis of the results reported in Table 13

38 The accession process imposes direct monetary and adjustment costs on the applicants. The process of preparing documents and reports demanded by the working parties is often a very expensive and time-consuming exercise that requires a high level of co-ordination in the public service. Other costs include the implementation of various administrative and sectoral reform measures that may be a precondition of a successful application for membership. In this section of the paper, however, we only consider the relatively higher number of commitments as the costs of accession negotiations.

39 Note that had we specified our equation in log-log form (i.e. logarithmic transformation of both the dependent and independent variables) β and θ would have been the constant elasticities with respect to income and exports. On the other hand, under the present specification, elasticity of C with respect to Y is given by $\beta(1/Y)$ and similarly with respect to X, $\theta(1/X)$. Obviously, unlike the case of log-log models, these elasticities will vary as Y and X change.

40 That the Gambia and Sierra Leone made commitments of unusually higher numbers was also revealed in an earlier section when cross-country comparisons were compared with per capita income.

41 This is known as Klein's rule of thumb (Gujarati, 1995).

42 These results can be made available on request.

43 While the significance of the coefficient on the dummy variable confirms that acceding countries are different from members, a positive sign on the coefficient implies that the average number of commitments for the former is higher than for the latter.

44 The mean difference is not significantly different from zero at the 5 per cent error probability level.

45 Furthermore, the construction of the 'import-weighted tariff' is usually performed at a relatively aggregated level, which may fail to take into account the variations in tariffs and import weights at a more disaggregated level.

46 Among others, Sach and Warner (1995), Edwards (1998) and Dollar and Kraay (2001) provide evidence of openness having a positive influence on economic growth, while Harrison and Hansen (1999) and Rodriguez and Rodrik (2001) suggest that such a direct relationship is not profound in a cross-country framework.

47 Raihan also uses two additional variables, a constructed 'distance' variable and foreign direct investment, in explaining the cross-country variation in TRB. However, since these two variables failed to register statistical significance, they have been excluded from the specification used in this paper.

48 Bulgaria applied for accession to the EU on 14 December 1995 and is expected to accede by 2007. Croatia applied on 21 February 2003, Estonia on 24 November 1995, Latvia on 13 October 1995 and

Lithuania on 8 December 1995. Of these, Estonia, Latvia and Lithuania have already acceded to the EU.

49 The statistical model for the analysis can be written as follows:

$$C_i = \alpha + \beta D_i + \delta D_2 + u_i$$

where C = number of commitments (or commitments made in sectors or sub-sectors at the 1-, 2- and 3-digit level of sectoral classification)

D_1 = 1 for all acceding countries except the five EU acceding countries. The variable controls for the EU accession requirements: WTO members as a whole have made more significant commitments than the WTO acceding countries.

D_2 = 1 for all EU acceding countries and 0 for all other countries.

D_1 and D_2 work together to remove any bias that might result in exhibiting differences in commitments between WTO members and acceding countries.

α is the intercept, β and δ are the slope coefficients and u is the error term. In that case, after estimating the equation, the following can be obtained (assuming that the mean of u is zero, i.e. $E(u) = 0$):

Mean commitments of WTO members = α

Mean commitment for WTO acceding countries excluding the EU acceding countries = $\alpha + \beta$

Mean commitment for EU acceding countries = $\alpha + \delta$

50 Finger and Schuler have estimated the cost of some of the proposed reforms in developing and transition economies. They find that in the case of customs valuation, various components of reform measures involve a cost of US$10 million per country; projects aimed at reforming sanitary and phyto-sanitary standards cost in the range of US$3.3–$112 million per country; and intellectual property rights cost US$4–$32.1 million per country. The estimates are based on the experience of World Bank projects in the countries concerned.

51 This point is made by Finger and Schuler (2000). While they discuss the issue with regard to least developed and transition economies within the WTO, it remains valid in the case of acceding countries.

References

Adlung, R., Carzeniga, A., Hoekman, B., Kono, M., Mattoo, A. and Tuthill, L. (2002), Chapter 27 in Hoekman, B., Mattoo, A. and English, P. (eds). *Development, Trade, and the WTO: A Handbook*, World Bank, pp. 259–79.

Adlung, R. (2000). 'Services Trade Liberalisation from Developed and Developing Country Perspectives', Chapter 5 in Sauve, P. and Stern, R.M. (eds). *GATS 2000: New Directions in Services Trade Liberalisation*. Brooking Institution Press, pp. 112–42.

Amsden, A.H. (2000). 'Selective Seclusion', in *The Rise of the Rest: Late Industrialization Outside the North Atlantic Economies*, manuscript.

Anderson, K. (1997). 'On the Complexities of China's WTO Accession', *The World Economy*, pp. 749–772.

Bhagwati, J.N. (1984). 'Splintering and Disembodiment of Services and Developing Nations', *The World Economy*, 7: 133–144.

Butkeviciene, J., Hayashi, M., Ognivtsev, V. and Yamaoka, T. (2002). 'Terms of WTO Accession', mimeo.

Broude, T. (1998). 'Accession to the WTO: Current Issues in the Arab World', *Journal of World Trade*, 32 (6): 147–66.

Dollar, D. and Kraay, A. (2002). 'Growth is Good for the Poor', *Journal of Economic Growth*, 7(3): 195–225. Reprinted in Shorrocks, A. and van der Hoeven, R. (eds) (2004). *Growth, Inequality, and Poverty*, Oxford: Oxford University Press for UNUWIDER.

Edwards, S. (1998). 'Openness, Productivity and Growth: What Do We Really Know?', *Economic Journal*, 108: 383–98.

Finger, M. and Schuer, P. (2000). 'Implementation of Uruguay Round Commitments: The Development Challenge', *The World Economy*, pp. 511–525.

Gallagher, P. (2000). *Guide to the WTO and Developing Countries*, Kluwer Law International and World Trade Organization.

Gylfason, T. (1999). 'Exports, Inflation and Growth', *World Development*, 27(6): 1031–57.

Grynberg, R. and Joy, M. (2000). 'The Accession of Vanuatu to the WTO: Lessons for the Multilateral Trading System', *Journal of World Trade*, 34: 159–73

Grynberg, R., Ognivtsev, V. and Razzaque, M. (2002). 'Paying the Price for Joining the WTO: A Comparative Assessment of Services Sector Commitments by WTO Members and Acceding Countries', Commonwealth Secretariat.

Harrison, A. (1996). 'Openness and Growth: A Time-Series, Cross-country Analysis for Developing Countries', *Journal of Development Economics*, 48: 419–447.

Harrison, A. and Hanson, G.H. (1999). 'Who Gains from Trade Reform? Some Remaining Puzzles', *Journal of Development Economics*, 59: 125–54.

Hoekman, B. (1996). 'Assessing the General Agreement on Trade in Services', Chapter 4 in Martin, W. and Winters, L.A. (eds). *The Uruguay Round and the Developing Countries*, Cambridge University Press.

Hoekman, B.M. and Kostecki, M.M. (2001). 'Trade in Services', Chapter 7 in *The Political Economy of the World Trading System: The WTO and Beyond*, Oxford University Press, pp. 237–273.

Jarque, C.M. and Bera, A.K. (1987). 'A Test for Normality of Observations and Regression Residuals', *International Statistical Review*, 55: 163–72.

Karsenty, G. (2000). 'Assessing Trade in Services by Mode of Supply', Chapter 2 in Sauve, P. and Stern, R.M. (eds), *GATS 2000:*

New Directions in Services Trade Liberalisation, Brooking Institution Press, pp. 33–56.

Langhammer, R.J. and Lucke, M. (2001). 'WTO Negotiations and Accession Issues for Vulnerable Economies', WIDER Discussion Paper No. 2001/36.

Lanoszka, A. (2001). 'The World Trade Organization Accession Process: Negotiating Participation in A Globalising Economy', *Journal of World Trade*, 35: 575–602.

Mattoo, A. (2000). 'Financial Services and the WTO': Liberalisation Commitments of the Developing and Transition Economies', *The World Economy*, 34: 351–86.

McCulloch, N., Winters, L.A. and Ciera, X. (2001). 'Trade in Services', Chapter 7 in *Trade Liberalisation and Poverty: A Handbook*, CEPR, pp. 229–52.

Mayda, A.M and Rodrik, D. (2001). 'Why Some People (and Countries) Are More Protectionist than Others', CEPR Discussion Paper 2960.

Ramsey, J.B. (1969). 'Tests for Specification Errors in Classical Linear Least Squares Regression Analysis', *Journal of the Royal Statistical Society*, series B, vol. 31: 350–71.

Rodriguez, F. and Rodrik, D (2000). 'Trade Policy and Economic Growth: A Skeptic's Guide to Cross National Evidence', *NBER Macroeconomics Annual*.

Sachs, J. and Warner, A. (1995). 'Economic Reforms and the Process of Global Integration', Brookings Papers on Economic Activity, pp. 1–95.

Sapir, A. (1999). 'The Geberal Agreement on Trade in Services: From 1994 to the Year 2000', *Journal of World Trade*, 33(1): 51–66.

Wei, Z. (1999). 'China's WTO Accession: Commitments and Prospects', *Journal of World Trade*, 33: 51–75.

Whichhard, O.G. (2001). 'Measurement, Classification, and Reporting of Services Activities: An International Perspective', mimeo.

White, H. (1980). 'A Heteroscedasticity Consistent Covariance Matrix Estimator and a Direct Test of Heteroscedasticity', *Econometrica*, 48: 817–18.

World Bank (1999). World Development Indicators CD-ROM 1999, World Bank, Washington, D.C.

WTO (2000). 'Technical Note on the Accession Process', Note prepared by the WTO Secretariat, WT/ACC/7/Rev.2, accessed from http://www.wto.org.

WTO (1999a). 'Recent Developments in Services Trade: Overview and Assessment', Background note prepared by the WTO Secretariat, S/C/W/94, 9 February 1999.

WTO (1999b). 'Structure of Commitments for Modes 1, 2, and 3', Background note prepared by the WTO Secretariat, S/C/W/99, Accessed from the website: http://www.wto.org on 22 February 2002.

WTO (1991). Services Sectoral Classification List, Note by the Secretariat, MTN.GTS/W/120, WTO, 10 July 1991.

UNCTAD (1967), The Question of the Granting and Extension of Preferences in Favour of Developing Countries, TD/B/C.2/AC/1/1, Geneva, May 31.

Yang, Y. (2000). 'China's WTO Accession: The Economics and Politics', *Journal of World Trade*, 34(4): 77–94.

Yang, W. (1999). 'Completing the WTO Accession Negotiations: Issues and Challenges', *The World Economy*, pp. 513–534.

Appendix 1

Services Sectoral Classification

1 Business Services

01.A. Professional Services
01.A.a. Legal Services
01.A.b. Accounting, Auditing and Bookeeping Services
01.A.c. Taxation Services
01.A.d. Architectural Services
01.A.e. Engineering Services
01.A.f. Integrated Engineering Services
01.A.g. Urban Planning and Landscape Architectural Services
01.A.h. Medical and Dental Services
01.A.i. Veterinary Services
01.A.j. Services Provided by Midwives, Nurses, Physiotherapists
01.A.k. Other

01.B. Computer and Related Services
01.B.a. Consultancy Services Related to the Installation of Computer
01.B.b. Software Implementation Services
01.B.c. Data Processing Services
01.B.d. Data Base Services
01.B.e. Other

01.C. Research and Development Services
01.C.a. R&D Services on Natural Sciences
01.C.b. R&D Services on Social Sciences and Humanities
01.C.c. Interdisciplinary R&D Services

01.D. Real Estate Services
01.D.a. Involving Own or Leased Property
01.D.b. On a Fee or Contract Basis

01.E. Rental/Leasing Services without Operators
01.E.a. Relating to Ships
01.E.b. Relating to Aircraft
01.E.c. Relating to other Transport Equipment
01.E.d. Relating to other Machinery and Equipment
01.E.e. Other

01.F. Other Business Services
01.F.a. Advertising Services
01.F.b. Market Research and Public Opinion Polling Services
01.F.c. Management Consulting Service
01.F.d. Services Related to Man. Consulting
01.F.e. Technical Testing and Analysis Services
01.F.f. Services Incidental to Agriculture, Hunting and Forestry
01.F.g. Services Incidental to Fishing
01.F.h. Services Incidental to Mining
01.F.i. Services Incidental to Manufacturing
01.F.j. Services Incidental to Energy Distribution
01.F.k. Placement and Supply Services of Personnel
01.F.l. Investigation and Security
01.F.m. Related Scientific and Technical Consulting Services
01.F.n. Maintenance and Repair of Equipment
01.F.o. Building-cleaning Services
01.F.p. Photographic Services
01.F.q. Packaging Services
01.F.r. Printing, Publishing
01.F.s. Convention Services
01.F.t. Other

2 Communication Services

02.A. Postal Services
02.B. Courier Services
02.C. Telecommunication Services
02.C.a. Voice Telephone Services
02.C.b. Packet-Switched Data Transmission Services
02.C.c. Circuit-Switched Data Transmission Services
02.C.d. Telex Services
02.C.e. Telegraph Services
02.C.f. Facsimile Services
02.C.g. Private Leased Circuit Services
02.C.h. Electronic Mail
02.C.i. Voice Mail
02.C.j. On-line Information and Data Base Retrieval
02.C.k. Electronic Data Interchange (EDI)
02.C.l. Enhanced/Value-Added Facsimile Services

02.C.m.Code and Protocol Conversion

02.C.n. On-line Information and/or data processing

02.C.o. Other Telecommunication Services

   02.C.o.01. Terrestrial based Mobile

   02.C.o.02. Satellite based Mobile

   02.C.o.03. Other

02.D. Audiovisual Services

02.D.a. Motion Picture and Video Tape Production and Distribution

02.D.b. Motion Picture Projection Service

02.D.c. Radio and Television Services

02.D.d. Radio and Television Transmission Services

02.D.e. Sound Recording

02.D.f. Other

02.E. Other

3 Construction and Related Engineering Services

03.A. General Construction Work for Building

03.B. General Construction work for Civil Engineering

03.C. Installation and Assembly Work

03.D. Building Completion and Finishing Work

03.E. Other

4 Distribution Services

04.A. Commission Agents' Services

04.B. Wholesale Trade Services

04.C. Retailing Services

04.D. Franchising

04.E. Other

5 Educational Services

05.A. Primary Education Services

05.B. Secondary Education Services

05.C. Higher Education Services

05.D. Adult Education

05.E. Other Education Services

6 Environmental Services

06.A. Sewage Services

06.B. Refuse Disposal Services

06.C. Sanitation and Similar Services

06.D. Other

7 Financial Services

07.A. All Insurance and Insurance-related Services

07.A.b. Reinsurance and Retrocession

07.A.c. Insurance Intermediation

07.A.a. Direct Insurance (including co-insurance)

   07.A.a.01.Life

   07.A.a.02 Non-life

07.A.d. Services Auxiliary to Insurance

07.B. Banking and Other Financial Services

07.B.a.Acceptance of deposits and other repayable funds

07.B.b. Lending of all types

07.B.c. Financial Leasing

07.B.d. All Payment and Money Transmission Services

07.B.e. Guarantees and Commitments

07.B.f. Trading for own account or for account of customers

   07.B.f.01. Money Market Instruments

   07.B.f.02. Foreign Exchange

   07.B.f.03. Derivative Products

   07.B.f.04. Exchange Rate and Interest Rate Instruments

   07.B.f.05. Transferable Securities

   07.B.f.06. Other negotiable instruments and financial assets

07.B.g. Participation in Issues of all Kinds of Securities

07.B.h. Money Broking

07.B.i. Asset Management

07.B.j. Settlement and Clearing Services for Financial Assets

07.B.k. Advisory and other Auxiliary Financial Services

07.B.l. Provision and Transfer of Financial Information

07.C. Other

8 Health Related and Social Services

08.A. Hospital Services

08.B. Other Human Health Services

08.C. Social Services

08.D. Other

9 Tourism and Travel Related Services

09.A. Hotels and Restaurants

09.B. Travel Agencies and Tour Operators Services

09.C. Tourist Guides Services

09.D. Other

10 Recreational, Cultural and Sporting Services

10.A. Entertainment Services

10.B. News Agency Services

10.C. Libraries, archives, museums and other cultural services

10.D. Sporting and Other Recreational Services

10.E. Other

11 Transport Services

11.A. Maritime Transport Services

11.A.a. Passenger Transportation

11.A.b. Freight Transportation

11.A.c. Rental of Vessels with Crew

11.A.d. Maintenance and Repair of Vessels

11.A.e. Pushing and Towing Services

11.A.f. Supporting Services for Maritime Transport

11.B. Internal Waterways Transport

11.B.a. Passenger Transportation

11.B.b. Freight Transportation

11.B.c. Rental of Vessels with Crew

11.B.d. Maintenance and Repair of Vessels

11.B.e. Pushing and Towing Services

11.B.f. Supporting Services for Internal Waterway Transport

11.C. Air Transport Services

11.C.a. Passenger Transportation

11.C.b. Freight Transportation

11.C.c. Rental of Aircraft with Crew

11.C.d. Maintenance and Repair of Aircraft

11.C.e. Supporting Services for Air Transport

11.D. Space Transport

11.E. Rail Transport Services

11.E.a. Passenger Transportation

11.E.b. Freight Transportation

11.E.c. Pushing and Towing Services

11.E.d. Maintenance and Repair of Rail Transport Equipment

11.E.e. Supporting Services for Rail Transport Services

11.F. Road Transport Services

11.F.a. Passenger Transportation

11.F.b. Freight Transportation

11.F.c. Rental of Commercial Vehicles with Operator

11.F.d. Maintenance and Repair of Road Transport Equipment

11.F.e. Supporting Services for Road Transport Services

11.G. Pipeline Transport

11.G.a. Transportation of Fuels

11.G.b. Transportation of other Goods

11.H. Services Auxiliary to All Modes of Transport

11.H.a. Cargo-handling Services

11.H.b. Storage and Warehouse Services

11.H.c. Freight Transport Agency Services

11.H.d. Other

11.I. Other Transport Services

12 Other Services not Included Elsewhere

Source: WTO Services Sectoral Classification List, MTN.GSN/W/120.

Appendix 2

Summary of Specific Commitments in the Services Sectors at the 1-digit Level

Countries	01.	02.	03.	04.	05.	06.	07.	08.	09.	10.	11.	12.	Total
Albania	X	X	X	X	X	X	X	X	X	X	X		11
Angola							X		X	X			3
Antigua and Barbuda	X	X					X		X	X	X		6
Argentina	X	X	X	X			X		X				6
Australia	X	X	X	X	X	X	X	X	X	X	X		11
Austria	X	X	X	X	X	X	X	X	X	X	X	X	12
Bahrain							X						1
Bangladesh		X							X				2
Barbados	X	X					X			X			4
Belize	X	X						X					3
Benin	X						X		X		X		4
Bolivia		X						X	X	X			4
Botswana	X	X							X				3
Brazil	X	X	X	X			X		X		X		7
Brunei Darussalam	X	X					X				X		4
Bulgaria	X	X	X	X	X	X	X	X	X	X	X		11
Burkina Faso									X				1
Burundi	X		X	X				X	X				5
Cameroon	X								X				2
Canada	X	X	X	X		X	X		X		X		8
Central African Rep.	X	X			X				X	X			5
Chad									X				1
Chile	X	X					X		X		X		5
China	X	X	X	X	X	X	X		X		X		9
Colombia	X	X	X			X	X		X				6
Congo									X	X			2
Congo RP	X	X	X		X				X	X			6
Costa Rica	X				X		X	X	X	X	X		7
Côte d'Ivoire	X	X	X				X		X		X		6
Croatia	X	X	X	X	X	X	X	X	X	X	X		11
Cuba	X	X	X				X		X	X	X		7
Cyprus	X	X					X						3
Czech Republic	X	X	X	X	X	X	X				X		9
Djibouti	X	X							X	X			4
Dominica		X					X		X	X			4
Dominican Republic	X	X	X				X	X	X				6
Ecuador	X	X	X	X		X	X		X	X	X		10
Egypt		X					X		X		X		4
El Salvador	X	X				X	X		X		X		6
Estonia	X	X	X	X	X	X	X	X	X	X	X		11
European Community	X	X	X	X	X	X	X	X	X	X	X	X	12
Fiji									X				1
Finland	X	X	X	X		X	X		X	X	X		9
Gabon	X		X				X		X				4
Gambia	X	X	X	X	X	X	X	X	X	X	X	X	12

| | Sectors | | | | | | | | | | | | |
Countries	01.	02.	03.	04.	05.	06.	07.	08.	09.	10.	11.	12.	Total
Georgia	X	X	X	X	X	X	X	X	X	X	X		11
Ghana		X	X		X		X		X		X		6
Grenada		X					X		X	X			4
Guatemala	X	X					X		X		X		5
Guinea	X					X		X	X		X		5
Guinea-Bissau									X	X			2
Guyana	X	X					X		X		X		5
Haiti	X		X		X		X		X				5
Honduras	X						X		X		X		4
Hong Kong	X	X	X	X			X		X	X	X		8
Hungary	X	X		X	X	X	X	X	X	X	X		10
Iceland	X	X	X	X		X	X		X	X	X		9
India	X	X	X				X	X	X				6
Indonesia	X	X	X				X		X		X		6
Israel	X	X				X	X		X				5
Jamaica	X	X			X		X	X	X	X	X		8
Japan	X	X	X	X	X	X	X		X	X	X		11
Jordan	X	X	X	X	X	X	X	X	X	X	X		11
Kenya		X					X		X		X	X	5
Korea RP	X	X	X	X		X	X		X		X		8
Kuwait	X		X	X		X	X	X	X	X			8
Kyrgyz Republic	X	X	X	X	X	X	X	X	X	X	X		11
Latvia	X	X	X	X	X	X	X	X	X	X	X		11
Lesotho	X	X	X	X	X	X	X		X		X	X	10
Liechtenstein	X	X		X	X	X	X		X	X	X		9
Lithuania	X	X	X	X	X	X	X	X	X	X	X		11
Macau	X						X		X				3
Madagascar	X												1
Malawi	X		X				X	X	X				5
Malaysia	X	X	X				X	X	X	X	X	X	9
Maldives	X												1
Mali						X			X				2
Malta							X		X		X		3
Mauritania									X				1
Mauritius		X					X		X				3
Mexico	X	X	X	X	X		X	X	X		X	X	10
Moldova	X	X	X	X	X	X	X	X	X	X	X		11
Mongolia	X	X	X	X			X		X				6
Morocco	X	X	X			X	X		X		X		7
Mozambique							X						1
Myanmar									X		X		2
Namibia	X								X				2
New Zealand	X	X	X	X	X		X		X		X		8
Nicaragua	X	X					X		X		X		5
Niger									X		X		2
Nigeria		X					X		X		X		4
Norway	X	X	X	X	X	X	X		X	X	X		10
Oman	X	X	X	X	X	X	X	X	X		X		10
Pakistan	X	X	X				X	X	X				6
Panama	X	X	X	X	X	X	X	X	X	X	X		11
Papua New Guinea	X	X	X				X		X		X		6
Paraguay							X		X				2

Countries	01.	02.	03.	04.	05.	06.	07.	08.	09.	10.	11.	12.	Total
							Sectors						
Peru	X	X		X			X		X	X	X		7
Philippines	X	X					X		X		X		5
Poland	X	X	X	X	X	X	X	X	X		X		10
Qatar	X	X	X			X	X		X				6
Romania	X	X	X	X			X	X	X		X		8
Rwanda	X				X	X			X	X			5
St Kitts & Nevis		X					X		X	X	X		5
St Lucia							X	X	X	X	X		5
St Vincent & Grenadines							X	X	X	X	X		5
Senegal	X	X		X			X		X	X	X		7
Sierra Leone	X	X	X		X	X	X	X	X	X	X		10
Singapore	X	X	X				X		X	X	X		7
Slovak Republic	X	X	X	X	X	X	X		X		X		9
Slovenia	X	X	X	X	X	X	X	X	X	X	X		11
Solomon Islands	X		X				X		X				4
South Africa	X	X	X	X		X	X		X		X	X	9
Sri Lanka		X					X		X				3
Suriname		X							X		X		3
Swaziland	X							X	X				3
Sweden	X	X	X	X		X	X		X	X	X		9
Switzerland	X	X	X	X	X	X	X		X	X	X		10
Taiwan	X	X	X	X	X	X	X	X	X	X	X		11
Tanzania									X				1
Thailand	X	X	X	X	X	X	X		X	X	X		10
Togo			X						X	X			3
Trinidad and Tobago	X	X	X		X		X	X	X	X	X		9
Tunisia		X					X		X				3
Turkey	X	X	X		X	X	X	X	X		X		9
Uganda		X							X				2
United Arab Emirates	X	X	X			X	X		X				6
Uruguay	X	X					X		X	X	X		6
USA	X	X	X	X	X	X	X	X	X	X	X		11
Venezuela	X	X	X				X		X	X	X	X	8
Zambia	X		X					X	X				4
Zimbabwe		X					X		X				3

Note: Shaded rows in bold are acceding countries. 'X' marks commitment(s) made in any specific sector. Any sector without 'X' indicates that a country has not made any commitment in that particular sector. The sectors are defined as:
01. Business Services
02. Communication Services
03. Construction and Related Engineering Services
04. Distribution Services
05. Educational Services
06. Environmental Services
07. Financial Services
08. Health Related and Social Services
09. Tourism and Travel Related Services
10. Recreational, Cultural and Sporting Services
11. Transport Services
12. Other Services not Included Elsewhere
Source: Except for China, Lithuania, Moldova and Taiwan data are from WTO. Commitments for these four countries are based on authors' own research.

Appendix 3

Commitments by Countries at the 2-digit Level

Sectors	01	02	03	04	05	06	07	08	09	10	11	ALL
Maximum Commitments	6	5	5	5	5	4	3	4	4	5	9	55
Countries						Commitments made in sectors						
Albania	4	5	5	4	4	4	2	2	3	4	4	41
Angola							1		1	1		3
Antigua and Barbuda	3	1					1		1	1	1	8
Argentina	3	2	4	3			3		4			19
Australia	6	1	4	4	3	3	2	1	3	2	5	34
Austria	6	2	5	4	3	4	2	3	3	4	4	40
Bahrain							2					2
Bangladesh		1							1			2
Barbados	2	2					1			1		6
Belize	1	1						1				3
Benin	1						1		1		2	5
Bolivia		1						1	2	3		7
Botswana	5	1							2			8
Brazil	2	2	4	3			2		1		4	18
Brunei Darussalam	3	1					2				1	7
Bulgaria	4	1	4	4	3	4	3	1	2	1	4	31
Burkina Faso									2			2
Burundi	2		5	3				2	3			15
Cameroon	1								2			3
Canada	6	2	5	5		4	2		2		5	31
Central Af. Rep.	1	1				1			4	4		11
Chad									2			2
Chile	3	1					3		3		1	11
China	4	3	5	5	5	4	3	0	2	0	6	37
Colombia	4	1	4			1	2		2			14
Congo									3	1		4
Congo RP	2	1	2		1				3	1		10
Costa Rica	3				3		1	1	3	1	1	13
Côte d'Ivoire	2	1	1				2		3		3	12
Croatia	6	2	5	4	4	4	2	3	4	3	6	43
Cuba	4	2	2				2		3	1	3	17
Cyprus	3	1					2					6
Czech Republic	5	2	5	3	5	3	2		3		4	32
Djibouti	1	3							1	1		6
Dominica		2					1		1	2		6
Dominican Republic	5	2	5				3	3	3			21
Ecuador	4	1	1	1		4	2	1	2	3	3	22
Egypt			3				3		4		1	11
El Salvador	4	2				1	2		3		1	13
Estonia	5	2	5	4	5	2	2	4	3	5	5	42
European Community	6	1	5	4	4	4	2	2	3	3	7	41
Fiji									1			1
Finland	6	1	3	4		2	2		3	2	6	29
Gabon	1		1				2		2			6

Sectors	01	02	03	04	05	06	07	08	09	10	11	ALL
Maximum Commitments	*6*	*5*	*5*	*5*	*5*	*4*	*3*	*4*	*4*	*5*	*9*	*55*
Countries						Commitments made in sectors						
Gambia	6	4	1	4	3	2	2	3	3	4	4	36
Georgia	6	3	5	4	4	4	2	3	2	4	5	42
Ghana		1	3		2		3		2		2	13
Grenada		2					1		1	2		6
Guatemala	1	1					2		4		1	9
Guinea	1					2		1	2		1	7
Guinea-Bissau									1	1		2
Guyana	1	1					2		2		2	8
Haiti	1		4		1		2		1			9
Honduras	2						2		3		2	9
Hong Kong	5	3	2	1			2		2	1	2	18
Hungary	5	1		3	4	2	2	4	2	2	7	32
Iceland	6	1	4	5		4	2		3	5	5	35
India	4	2	1				2	1	2			12
Indonesia	4	1	4				2		3		1	15
Israel	3	4				4	2		3			16
Jamaica	5	1			3		1	1	2	1	2	16
Japan	6	2	5	4	4	4	2	1	3	4	8	43
Jordan	6	3	5	5	5	2	2	3	2	4	3	40
Kenya		2					2		3		2	9
Korea RP	5	2	5	4		3	3		3		5	30
Kuwait	4		4	3		3	1	3	3	2		23
Kyrgyz Republic	6	4	5	4	4	4	2	4	4	5	6	48
Latvia	5	2	5	4	4	4	2	2	4	2	5	39
Lesotho	5	3	4	3	5	4	2		3		1	30
Liechtenstein	5	1		4	4	4	2		3	2	2	27
Lithuania	5	2	5	4	4	4	2	2	2	4	7	41
Macau	1						2		2			5
Madagascar	1											1
Malawi	2		5				1	2	4			14
Malaysia	5	2	5				2	1	2	2	2	21
Maldives	2											2
Mali				1					1			2
Malta							2		2		1	5
Mauritania									3			3
Mauritius		1					2		4			7
Mexico	5	3	4	2	4		3	2	3		4	30
Moldova	6	3	5	5	5	4	2	3	4	5	8	50
Mongolia	2	3	2	2			2		3			14
Morocco	3	1	5			4	2		4		2	21
Mozambique							1		2			3
Myanmar											3	3
Namibia	1								2			3
New Zealand	5	2	5	3	3		2		3		6	29
Nicaragua	3	2					2		3		2	12
Niger									3		3	6
Nigeria		1					2		3		2	8
Norway	6	2	5	3	5	4	2		3	1	5	36
Oman	3	3	5	4	4	4	2	1	2		3	31
Pakistan	4	1	1				2	1	2			11
Panama	4	2	4	3	3	1	2	1	2	1	1	24

Sectors	01	02	03	04	05	06	07	08	09	10	11	ALL
Maximum Commitments	*6*	*5*	*5*	*5*	*5*	*4*	*3*	*4*	*4*	*5*	*9*	*55*
Countries						Commitments made in sectors						
Papua New Guinea	3	2	2				1		1		1	10
Paraguay							2		3			5
Peru	3	1		2			2		2	2	2	14
Philippines	2	2					2		2		5	13
Poland	3	2	5	2	4	1	2	1	2		1	23
Qatar	4	1	4			4	2		1			16
Romania	3	1	4	3		1	2		3		2	19
Rwanda	1			1	1				1	1		5
St Kitts & Nevis		1					1		1	2	1	6
St Lucia							1	1	1	2	2	7
St Vincent & Grenadines							1	1	1	2	2	7
Senegal	2	3		2			2		2	1	1	13
Sierra Leone	3	1	5		5	4	2	4	4	3	5	36
Singapore	4	3	5				2		3	1	2	20
Slovak Republic	5	2	5	3	5	3	2		3		4	32
Slovenia	5	2	5	4	3	4	2	2	2	1	5	35
Solomon Islands	1		2				2		1			6
South Africa	5	2	4	3		4	2		3		1	24
Sri Lanka		1					2		2			5
Suriname		1							2		1	4
Swaziland	4							1	1			6
Sweden	6	1	5	3		4	2		3	3	3	30
Switzerland	5	1	5	4	4	4	2		3	2	6	36
Taiwan	6	3	5	4	4	2	3	1	3	2	4	37
Tanzania									1			1
Thailand	4	2	3	1	3	4	2		3	1	5	28
Togo			1						3	1		5
Trinidad and Tobago	4	1	1		2		1	1	2	2	1	15
Tunisia		1					2		2			5
Turkey	3	3	4		4	3	2	1	2		4	26
Uganda		1							2			3
United Arab Emirates	4	1	5			4	1		2			17
Uruguay	4	1					1		3	1	1	11
USA	5	3	5	4	2	4	2	1	4	4	4	38
Venezuela	5	2	5				2		3	2	2	21
Zambia	2		5					2	4			13
Zimbabwe		1					1		3			5
Total	343	159	256	146	131	145	187	74	292	118	232	2083

Note: Description of sectoral classification is given in Appendix 1. Data for China, Lithuania, Moldova and Taiwan are taken from the authors' own research employing similar methodology, while data for all other countries are from the WTO.

Appendix 4

Commitments by Countries at the Most Disaggregated Level

Sectors	1	2	3	4	5	6	7	8	9	10	11	Total
Maximum number	*46*	*26*	*5*	*5*	*5*	*4*	*23*	*4*	*4*	*5*	*35*	*162*
Albania	31	26	5	4	4	4	22	2	3	4	15	120
Angola	3	0					3		1	1	0	8
Antigua and Barbuda	9	17					1		1	1	2	31
Argentina	16	17	4	3			20		4		0	64
Australia	35	14	4	4	3	3	21	1	3	2	13	103
Austria	43	16	5	4	3	4	21	3	3	4	6	112
Bahrain	0	0					21				0	21
Bangladesh	0	10					0		1		0	11
Barbados	3	18					1			1	0	23
Belize	1	17					0	1			0	19
Benin	1	0					3		1		7	12
Bolivia	0	9					0	1	2	3	0	15
Botswana	16	1					0		2		0	19
Brazil	10	17	4	3			19		1		5	59
Brunei Darussalam	8	8					5				1	22
Bulgaria	27	13	4	4	3	4	14	1	2	1	7	80
Burkina Faso	0	0					0		2		0	2
Burundi	9	0	5	3			0	2	3		0	22
Cameroon	1	0					0		2		0	3
Canada	35	17	5	5		4	21		2		15	104
Central Af. Rep.	2	6				1	0		4	4	0	17
Chad	0	0					0		2		0	2
Chile	8	12					15		3		2	40
China	25	11	5	5	5	4	13	0	2	0	15	85
Colombia	18	15	4			1	18		2		0	58
Congo	0	0					0		3	1	0	4
Congo RP	4	1	2		1		0		3	1	0	12
Costa Rica	6	0			3		5	1	3	1	1	20
Côte d'Ivoire	3	10	1				6		3		7	30
Croatia	39	17	5	4	4	4	21	3	4	3	20	124
Cuba	6	8	2				21		3	1	7	48
Cyprus	7	9					9				0	25
Czech Republic	27	11	5	3	5	3	19		3		10	86
Djibouti	1	12					0		1	1	0	15
Dominica	0	18					1		1	2	0	22
Dominican Republic	29	12	5				10	3	3		0	62
Ecuador	16	9	1	1		4	19	1	2	3	9	65
Egypt	0	0	3				18		4		3	28
El Salvador	8	11				1	7		3		1	31
Estonia	28	18	5	4	5	2	21	4	3	5	8	103
European Community	42	14	5	4	4	4	21	2	3	3	13	115
Fiji	0	0					0		1		0	1
Finland	37	14	3	4		2	21		3	2	12	98
Gabon	1	0	1				14		2		0	18
Gambia	37	17	1	4	3	2	18	3	3	4	17	109

Sectors	1	2	3	4	5	6	7	8	9	10	11	Total
Maximum number	*46*	*26*	*5*	*5*	*5*	*4*	*23*	*4*	*4*	*5*	*35*	*162*
Georgia	41	22	5	4	4	4	20	3	2	4	17	126
Ghana	0	10	3		2		9		2		4	30
Grenada	0	17					1		1	2	0	21
Guatemala	2	9					3		4		2	20
Guinea	1	0				2	2	1	2		3	11
Guinea-Bissau	0	0					0		1	1	0	2
Guyana	5	1					3		2		5	16
Haiti	1	0	4		1		9		1		0	16
Honduras	3	0					7		3		3	16
Hong Kong	19	19	2	1			18		2	1	6	68
Hungary	37	17		3	4	2	21	4	2	2	11	103
Iceland	39	14	4	5		4	21		3	5	16	111
India	8	11	1				14	1	2		0	37
Indonesia	11	11	4				15		3		2	46
Israel	18	16				4	17		3		0	58
Jamaica	19	17			3		4	1	2	1	2	49
Japan	32	17	5	4	4	4	21	1	3	4	15	110
Jordan	35	21	5	5	5	2	20	3	2	4	8	110
Kenya	0	19					11		3		7	40
Korea RP	31	18	5	4		3	22		3		10	96
Kuwait	26	0	4	3		3	17	3	3	2	0	61
Kyrgyz Republic	39	24	5	4	4	4	19	4	4	5	27	139
Latvia	37	22	5	4	4	4	21	2	4	2	21	126
Lesotho	34	7	4	3	5	4	11		3		3	74
Liechtenstein	32	9		4	4	4	21		3	2	7	86
Lithuania	37	16	5	4	4	4	21	2	2	4	14	113
Macau	1	0					21		2		0	24
Madagascar	2	0					0				0	2
Malawi	5	0	5				17	2	4		0	33
Malaysia	24	17	5				19	1	2	2	4	74
Maldives	5	0					0				0	5
Mali	0	0			1		0		1		0	2
Malta	0	0					7		2		2	11
Mauritania	0	0					0		3		0	3
Mauritius	0	10					14		4		0	28
Mexico	24	18	4	2	4		15	2	3		5	77
Moldova	45	17	5	5	5	4	16	3	4	5	34	143
Mongolia	6	9	2	2			14	0	3		0	36
Morocco	5	12	5			4	11		4		4	45
Mozambique	0	0					17		2		0	19
Myanmar	0	0					0				3	3
Namibia	1	0					0		2		0	3
New Zealand	20	21	5	3	3		21		3		13	89
Nicaragua	13	15					10		3		8	49
Niger	0	0					0		3		4	7
Nigeria	0	10					15		3		4	32
Norway	38	15	5	3	5	4	21		3	1	16	111
Oman	29	20	5	4	4	4	16	1	2		7	92
Pakistan	11	12	1				19	1	2		0	46
Panama	23	12	4	3	3	1	18	1	2	1	1	69
Papua New Guinea	6	10	2				7		1		2	28
Paraguay	0	0					5		3		0	8

Sectors	1	2	3	4	5	6	7	8	9	10	11	Total
Maximum number	46	26	5	5	5	4	23	4	4	5	35	162
Peru	7	15		2			20		2	2	2	50
Philippines	3	12					19		2		14	50
Poland	17	16	5	2	4	1	12	1	2		2	62
Qatar	15	1	4			4	21		1		0	46
Romania	11	16	4	3		1	15		3		4	57
Rwanda	2	0			1	1	0		1	1	0	6
St Kitts & Nevis	0	3					1		1	2	1	8
St Lucia	0	0					1	1	1	2	3	8
St Vincent & Grenadines	0	0					1	1	1	2	3	8
Senegal	4	13		2			7		2	1	1	30
Sierra Leone	36	1	5		5	4	21	4	4	3	26	109
Singapore	20	14	5				21		3	1	2	66
Slovak Republic	27	18	5	3	5	3	20		3		10	94
Slovenia	26	6	5	4	3	4	21	2	2	1	8	82
Solomon Islands	4	0	2				21		1		0	28
South Africa	36	16	4	3		4	21		3		3	90
Sri Lanka	0	6					19		2		0	27
Suriname	0	9					0		2		2	13
Swaziland	7	0					0	1	1		0	9
Sweden	38	14	5	3		4	21		3	3	6	97
Switzerland	37	16	5	4	4	4	21		3	2	19	115
Taiwan	40	18	5	4	4	2	18	1	3	2	13	110
Tanzania	0	0					0		1		0	1
Thailand	21	10	3	1	3	4	16		3	1	12	74
Togo	0	0	1				0		3	1	0	5
Trinidad and Tobago	9	14	1		2		1	1	2	2	2	34
Tunisia	0	6					13		2		0	21
Turkey	13	19	4		4	3	21	1	2		10	77
Uganda	0	5					0		2		0	7
United Arab Emirates	18	1	5			4	16		2		0	46
Uruguay	15	1					3		3	1	1	24
USA	34	24	5	4	2	4	21	1	4	4	8	111
Venezuela	21	8	5				21		3	2	3	63
Zambia	5	0	5				0	2	4		0	16
Zimbabwe	0	13					8		3		0	24

Note: Descriptions of the sectors are given in Appendix 1.

Appendix 5

Cross-country Relationship between PPP GDP Per Capita and Number of Commitments at the 3-digit Level

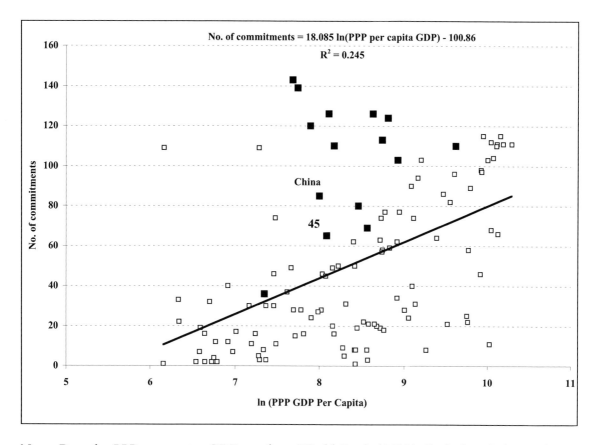

Note: Data for PPP per capita GDP are from World Bank (1999). Barbados, Cuba, Djibouti, Kuwait, Liechtenstein, Macau, Namibia, Oman, Qatar, Rwanda and Suriname are deleted due to lack of data on PPP per capita GDP. For Taiwan the figures for PPP GDP per capita are approximated by those for Korea. Since Oman is excluded, 15 acceding countries are represented in the figure.

Appendix 6

Cross-country Relationship between Export-GDP Ratio and Number of Commitments at the 3-digit Level

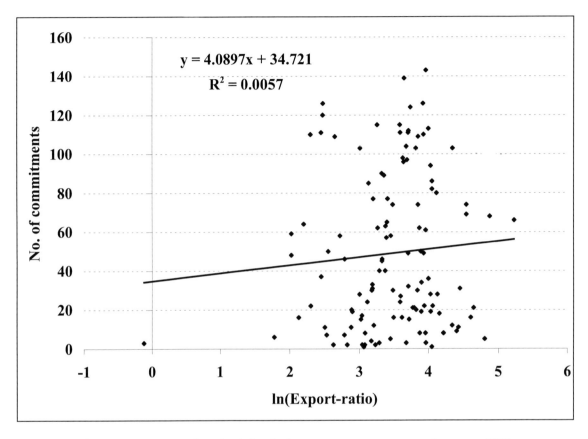

Note: Based on 124 countries for which both data on commitments and export-GDP ratio were available. Data on export-GDP ratio are from the *World Bank World Development Indicators 1999* (World Bank, 1999) and are mostly for 1997.

Appendix 7

Actual less Predicted Commitments at the 3-digit Level based on All Countries in the Regression Mode (Column 4 under 3-digit level commitments in Table 13)

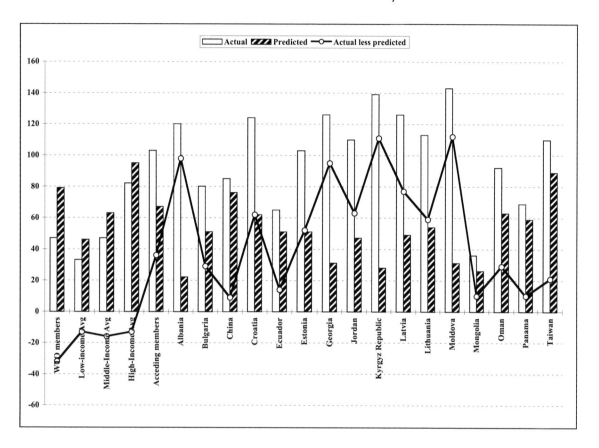

Appendix 8

Actual less Predicted Commitments at the 3-digit Level based on Regression Coefficient Excluding Acceding Countries and EC as a Single Unit

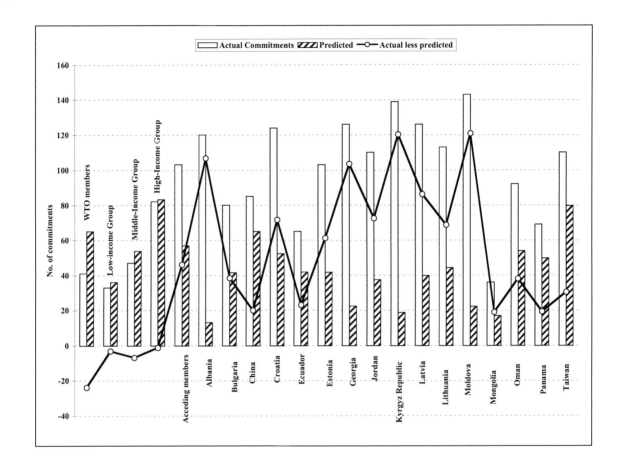

AN EVALUATION OF THE TERMS OF ACCESSION TO THE WORLD TRADE ORGANIZATION

Appendix 9

Actual Less Predicted Commitments at the 3-digit Level based on All Countries in the Regression Model and EC as a Single Unit

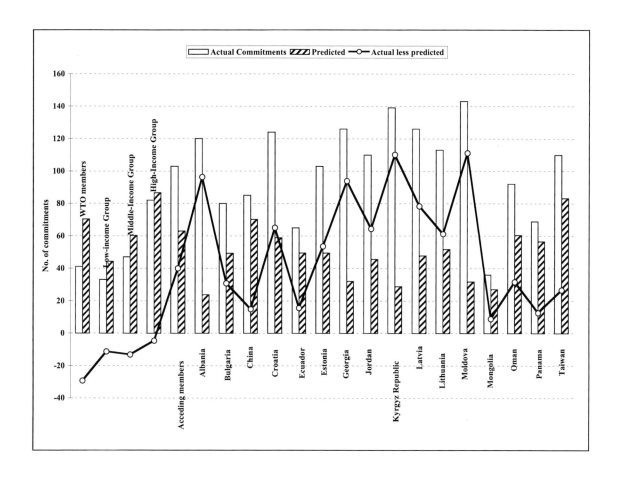